Chinese-English edition

中英文对照

CONFUCIUS

The Analects

论语

杨伯峻 今译 刘殿爵 英译

Translated by

Yang Bojun (Modern Chinese)

D.C. Lau (English)

中華書局

ZHONGHUA BOOK COMPANY

图书在版编目(CIP)数据

论语:汉英对照/(春秋)孔丘著;杨伯峻今译;刘殿爵英译.—北京:中华书局,2008.8(2009.5重印)
ISBN 978-7-101-06228-1

Ⅰ.论…　Ⅱ.①孔…②杨…③刘…　Ⅲ.①儒家②论语-译文-汉、英　Ⅳ.B222.24

中国版本图书馆CIP数据核字(2008)第109216号

书　　名　论语(中英文对照)
今 译 者　杨伯峻
英 译 者　刘殿爵
责任编辑　张继海　王瑞玲
出版发行　中华书局
　　　　　(北京市丰台区太平桥西里38号　100073)
　　　　　http://www.zhbc.com.cn
　　　　　E-mail:zhbc@zhbc.com.cn
印　　刷　北京市白帆印务有限公司
版　　次　2008年8月北京新1版
　　　　　2009年5月北京第3次印刷
规　　格　开本/787×1092毫米　1/32
　　　　　印张12　插页2　字数250千字
印　　数　8001-11000册
国际书号　ISBN 978-7-101-06228-1
定　　价　36.00元

出版说明

《论语》是中国人的经典。不仅如此，在日本、朝鲜半岛、越南等传统汉文化圈内，千百年来，《论语》也是广为人们传诵和学习的中国典籍之一。随着近代以来中外交流的日益密切，《论语》更成为具有世界意义的经典，集中代表了东方儒家文化的思想智慧。西方人也好，东方人也罢，欲了解中国的传统，了解中国人的精神世界与思想本源，就必须阅读《论语》。

进入21世纪，中国的发展与崛起引来全球的瞩目，中华文化也从未像今天这样受到国际社会如此的重视。《论语》——这部承载了厚重文化积淀的传统经典，正重现勃勃生机，在海外知识界与普通读者中获得了空前的关注。为此我们决定出版中外文对照本的《论语》，以满足中文世界之外的更广大范围内的阅读需求。

继不久前推出中日文对照本《论语》之后，我们这次推出了中英文对照本《论语》。它包括《论语》原文、中文今译和英文今译三部分。《论语》原文和中文今译我们依据的是最权威的杨伯峻先生的译本，英文今译则选用了企鹅出版集团出版的著名学者刘殿爵（D. C. Lau）先生的译本。刘殿爵先生在伦敦大学执教近 30 年，在西方汉学界享有很高声望。他的译本被誉为具有里程碑的意义，已经成为长销不衰的“企鹅经典”。需要说明的是，对于《论语》原文的理解，杨、刘二位先生偶尔会有差异。这些地方我们均保留原貌，用斜体字表示，敬希读者注意。

中华书局编辑部

二〇〇八年七月

Note on New Bilingual Edition

I have taken the opportunity of this new bilingual edition to give the translation a thorough revision. The revisions are of two kinds. First, there are cases where I have made changes in the interpretation of the original text. Second, there are passages where I have tightened the translation. In this respect I think elegance should give place to accuracy wherever there is conflict between the two.

I must thank Professor D. E. Pollard of the School of Oriental and African Studies who happened to be visiting The Chinese University of Hong Kong for his kindness in reading the revised translation and giving valuable advice.

Hong Kong D.C.L.
April 1988

目录

CONTENTS

The Analects of Confucius

The Analects of Confucius

(Lun yu)

学而篇第一

1. 子曰："学而时习之，不亦说乎?有朋自远方来，不亦乐乎?人不知，而不愠，不亦君子乎?"

孔子说："学了，然后按一定的时间去实习它，不也高兴吗？有志同道合的人从远处来，不也快乐吗？人家不了解我，我却不怨恨，不也是君子吗？"

2. 有子曰："其为人也孝弟，而好犯上者，鲜矣；不好犯上，而好作乱者，未之有也。君子务本，本立而道生。孝弟也者，其为仁之本与!"

有子说："他的为人，孝顺爹娘，敬爱兄长，却喜欢触犯上级，这种人是很少的；不喜欢触犯上级，却喜欢造反，这种人从来没有过。君子专心致力于基础工作，基础树立了，'道'就会产生。孝顺爹娘，敬爱兄长，这就是'仁'的基础吧！"

3. 子曰："巧言令色，鲜矣仁!"

孔子说："花言巧语，伪善的面貌，这种人，'仁德'是不会多的。"

4. 曾子曰："吾日三省吾身——为人谋而不忠乎？与朋友交而不信乎?传不习乎?"

BOOK 1

1. The Master said, "Is it not a pleasure, having learned something, to try it out at due intervals? Is it not a joy to have like-minded friends come from afar? Is it not gentlemanly not to take offence when others fail to appreciate your abilities?"[1]

1. Cf. XIV.30, XV.19.

2. You Zi said, "It is rare for a man whose character is such that he is good as a son and obedient as a young man to have the inclination to transgress against his superiors; it is unheard of for one who has no such inclination to be inclined to start a rebellion. The gentleman devotes his efforts to the roots, for once the roots are established, the Way will grow therefrom. Being good as a son and obedient as a young man is, perhaps, the root of *a man's character.*"

3. The Master said, "It is rare, indeed, for a man with cunning words and an ingratiating countenance to be benevolent."[2]

2. Part of this saying is also found in V.25.

4. Zeng Zi said, "Every day I examine myself on three counts. In what I have undertaken on another's behalf, have I failed to do

曾子说："我每天多次自己反省:替别人办事是否尽心竭力了呢？同朋友往来是否诚实呢？老师传授我的学业是否复习了呢？"

5. 子曰："道千乘之国，敬事而信，节用而爱人，使民以时。"

孔子说："治理具有一千辆兵车的国家，就要严肃认真地对待工作，信实无欺，节约费用，爱护官吏，役使老百姓要在农闲时间。"

6. 子曰："弟子，入则孝，出则悌，谨而信，泛爱众，而亲仁。行有余力，则以学文。"

孔子说："后生小子，在父母跟前，就孝顺父母；离开自己房子，便敬爱兄长；寡言少语，说则诚实可信，博爱大众，亲近有仁德的人。这样躬行实践之后，有剩余力量，就再去学习文献。"

7. 子夏曰："贤贤易色；事父母，能竭其力；事君，能致其身；与朋友交，言而有信。虽曰未学，吾必谓之学矣。"

子夏说："对妻子，重品德，不重容貌；侍奉爹娘，能尽

my best? In my dealings with my friends have I failed to be trustworthy in what I say? Have I failed to practise repeatedly what has been passed on to me?"

5. The Master said, "In guiding a state of a thousand chariots, approach your duties with reverence and be trustworthy in what you say; keep expenditure under proper regulation and love your fellow men; employ the labour of the common people in the right seasons."

6. The Master said, "A young man should be a good son at home and an obedient young man abroad, sparing of speech but trustworthy in what he says, and should love the multitude at large but *cultivate the friendship of his fellow men*.[3] If, after all these activities, he has any energy to spare, let him use it to making himself cultivated."

3. For the contrast of *ren* (fellow men) with *zhong* (multitude) see XVII.6.

7. Zi-xia said, "I would grant that a man is, indeed, schooled who shows deference to men of excellence by putting on the right countenance, who exerts himself to the utmost in the service of

心竭力；服事君上，能豁出生命；同朋友交往，说话诚实守信。这种人，虽说没学习过，我一定说他已经学习过了。”

8. 子曰：“君子不重，则不威；学则不固。主忠信。无友不如己者。过，则勿惮改。”

孔子说：“君子，如果不庄重，就没有威严；即使读书，所学的也不会巩固。要以忠和信两种道德为主。不要跟不如自己的人交朋友。有了过错，就不要怕改正。”

9. 曾子曰：“慎终，追远，民德归厚矣。”

曾子说：“谨慎地对待父母的死亡，追念远代祖先，自然会导致老百姓归于忠厚老实了。”

10. 子禽问于子贡曰：“夫子至于是邦也，必闻其政，求之与？抑与之与？”

his parents and offers his person to the service of his lord, and who, in his dealings with his friends, is trustworthy in what he says, even though he be said to be unschooled."

8. The Master said, "A gentleman who lacks gravity does not inspire awe. A gentleman who studies is unlikely to be inflexible.

"Make[4] it your guiding principle to do your best for others and to be trustworthy in what you say. Do not accept as friend anyone who is not as good as you.

"When you make a mistake, do not be afraid of mending your ways."

4. The whole of what follows is found also in IX.25 while the opening sentence is found also in XII. 10.

9. Zeng Zi said, "Conduct the funeral of your parents with meticulous care and let not sacrifices to your remote ancestors be forgotten, and the virtue of the common people will incline towards fullness."

10. Zi-qin asked Zi-gong, When the Master arrives in a state, he invariably gets to know about its government. Does he seek this

子贡曰："夫子温、良、恭、俭、让以得之。夫子之求之也，其诸异乎人之求之与？"

子禽向子贡问道："他老人家一到哪个国家，必然听得到那个国家的政事，求来的呢？还是别人自动告诉他的呢？"

子贡道："他老人家是靠温和、善良、严肃、节俭、谦逊来取得的。他老人家获得的方法，和别人获得的方法，不相同吧？"

11. 子曰："父在，观其志；父没，观其行；三年无改于父之道，可谓孝矣。"

孔子说："当他父亲活着，〔因为他无权独立行动，〕要观察他的志向；他父亲死了，要考察他的行为；若是他对他父亲的合理部分，长期地不加改变，可以说做到孝了。"

12. 有子曰："礼之用，和为贵。先王之道，斯为美；小大由之。有所不行，知和而和，不以礼节之，亦不可行也。"

有子说："礼的作用，以遇事都做得恰当为可贵。过去圣明君王的治理国家，可宝贵的地方就在这里；他们小事大事都做得恰当。但是，如有行不通的地方，便为恰当而求恰当，不用一定的规矩制度来加以节制，也是不可行的。"

information? or is it given him?"

Zi-gong said, "The Master gets it through being cordial, wellbehaved, respectful, frugal and deferential. The way the Master seeks it is, perhaps, different from the way other men seek it."

11. The Master said, "Observe what a man has in mind to do when his father is living, and then observe what he does when his father is dead. If, for three years, he makes no changes to his father's ways, he can be said to be a good son."[5]

5. This sentence is found again in IV.20. Cf. also XIX. 18.

12. You Zi said, "Of the things brought about by the rites, harmony is the most valuable. Of the ways of the Former Kings, this is the most beautiful, and is followed alike in matters great and small, yet this will not always work: to aim always at harmony without regulating it by the rites simply because one knows only about harmony will not, in fact, work."

13. 有子曰：“信近于义，言可复也。恭近于礼，远耻辱也。因不失其亲，亦可宗也。”

有子说：“所守的约言符合义，说的话就能兑现。态度容貌的庄矜合于礼，就不致遭受侮辱。依靠关系深的人，也就可靠了。”

14. 子曰：“君子食无求饱，居无求安，敏于事而慎于言，就有道而正焉，可谓好学也已。”

孔子说：“君子，吃食不要求饱足，居住不要求舒适，对工作勤劳敏捷，说话却谨慎，到有道的人那里去匡正自己，这样，可以说是好学了。”

15. 子贡曰：“贫而无谄，富而无骄，何如？”

子曰：“可也；未若贫而乐，富而好礼者也。”

13. You Zi said, "To be trustworthy in word is close to being moral in that it enables one's words to be repeated.[6] To be respectful is close to being observant of the rites in that it enables one to stay clear of disgrace and insult. *If, in promoting good relationship with relatives by marriage, a man manages not to lose the good will of his own kinsmen, he is worthy of being looked up to as the head of the clan.*"[7]

6. For a discussion of the interpretation of this sentence see D. C. Lau, "On the Expression *Fu Yen*".

7. The sense of this last sentence is rather obscure. The present translation, though tentative, is based on a comment of Zheng Xuan's on the word *yin* in the *Zhou li* (*Zhou li zhu shu*, 10.24b).

14. The Master said, "The gentleman seeks neither a full belly nor a comfortable home. He is quick in action but cautious in speech.[8] He goes to men possessed of the Way to have himself put right. Such a man can be described as eager to learn."

8. Cf. IV.24.

15. Zi-gong said, "'Poor without being obsequious, wealthy without being arrogant.' What do you think of this saying?"

子贡曰："《诗》云：'如切如磋，如琢如磨'，其斯之谓与？"

子曰："赐也，始可与言《诗》已矣，告诸往而知来者。"

子贡说："贫穷却不巴结奉承，有钱却不骄傲自大，怎么样？"

孔子说："可以了；但是还不如虽贫穷却乐于道，纵有钱却谦虚好礼哩。"

子贡说："《诗经》上说：'要像对待骨、角、象牙、玉石一样，先开料，再糙锉，细刻，然后磨光。'那就是这样的意思吧？"

孔子道："赐呀，现在可以同你讨论《诗经》了，告诉你一件，你能有所发挥，举一反三了。"

16. 子曰："不患人之不己知，患不知人也。"

孔子说："别人不了解我，我不急；我急的是自己不了解别人。"

The Master said, "That will do, but better still 'Poor yet delighting in the Way, wealthy yet observant of the rites.'"

Zi-gong said, "The *Odes* say,

Like bone cut, like horn polished,

Like jade carved, like stone ground.

Is not what you have said a case in point?"

The Master said, "Ci, only with a man like you can one discuss the *Odes*. Tell such a man something and he can see its relevance to what he has not been told."

16. The Master said, "It is not the failure of others to appreciate your abilities that should trouble you, but rather your failure to appreciate theirs.

为政篇第二

1. 子曰："为政以德，譬如北辰居其所而众星共之。"

孔子说："用道德来治理国政，自己便会像北极星一般，在一定的位置上，别的星辰都环绕着它。"

2. 子曰："《诗》三百，一言以蔽之，曰：'思无邪'。"

孔子说："《诗经》三百篇，用一句话来概括它，就是'思想纯正'。"

3. 子曰："道之以政，齐之以刑，民免而无耻；道之以德，齐之以礼，有耻且格。"

孔子说："用政法来诱导他们，使用刑罚来整顿他们，人民只是暂时地免于罪过，却没有廉耻之心。如果用道德来诱导他们，使用礼教来整顿他们，人民不但有廉耻之心，而且人心归服。"

4. 子曰："吾十有五而志于学，三十而立，四十而不惑，五十而知天命，六十而耳顺，七十而从心所欲，不逾矩。"

孔子说："我十五岁，有志于学问；三十岁，[懂礼仪，]说话做事都有把握；四十岁，[掌握了各种知识，]不致迷

BOOK 2

1. The Master said, "The rule of virtue can be compared to the Pole Star which commands the homage of the multitude of stars simply by remaining in its place."

2. The Master said, "The *Odes* are three hundred in number. They can be summed up in one phrase,

   Swerving not from the right path."[1]

1. This line is from Ode 297 where it describes a team of horses going straight ahead without swerving to left or right.

3. The Master said, "Guide them by edicts, keep them in line with punishments, and the common people will stay out of trouble but will have no sense of shame. Guide them by virtue, keep them in line with the rites, and they will, besides having a sense of shame, reform themselves."

4. The Master said, "At fifteen I set my heart on learning; at thirty I took my stand;[2] at forty I was never in two minds;[3] at fifty I understood the Decree of Heaven; at sixty my ear was attuned;[4] at seventy I followed my heart's desire without overstepping the

惑；五十岁，得知天命；六十岁，一听别人言语，便可以分别真假，判明是非；到了七十岁，便随心所欲，任何念头不越出规矩。”

5. 孟懿子问孝。子曰：“无违。”

樊迟御，子告之曰：“孟孙问孝于我，我对曰，无违。”

樊迟曰：“何谓也？”

子曰：“生，事之以礼；死，葬之以礼，祭之以礼。”

孟懿子向孔子问孝道。孔子说：“不要违背礼节。”

不久，樊迟替孔子赶车子，孔子便告诉他说：“孟孙向我问孝道，我答复说，不要违背礼节。”

樊迟道：“这是什么意思？”

孔子道：“父母活着，依规定的礼节侍奉他们；死了，依规定的礼节埋葬他们，祭祀他们。”

6. 孟武伯问孝。子曰：“父母唯其疾之忧。”

孟武伯向孔子请教孝道。孔子道：“做爹娘的只是为孝子

line."

2. on the rites. Cf. VIII.8, XVI. 13, XX.3.

3. Cf. IX.29, XIV.28.

4. The expression *er shun* is very obscure and the translation is tentative. It is worth pointing out that the graph 聖 (sage) has an 耳 (ear) component, and this saying of Confucius' may have some bearing on the fact that he was regarded as a sage by even his contemporaries (see, e.g., IX.6).

5. Meng Yi Zi asked about being filial. The Master answered, "Never fail to comply."

Fan Chi was driving. The Master told him about the interview, saying, "Meng-sun asked me about being filial. I answered, 'Never fail to comply.'"

Fan Chi asked, "What does that mean?"

The Master said, "When your parents are alive, comply with the rites in serving them; when they die, comply with the rites in burying them and in offering sacrifices to them."

6. Meng Wu Bo asked about being filial. The Master said, "Give your father and mother no cause for anxiety other than illness."

的疾病发愁。”

7. 子游问孝。子曰：“今之孝者，是谓能养。至于犬马，皆能有养；不敬，何以别乎？”

子游问孝道。孔子说：“现在的所谓孝，就是说能够养活爹娘便行了。至于狗马都能够得到饲养；若不存心严肃地孝顺父母，那养活爹娘和饲养狗马怎样去分别呢？”

8. 子夏问孝。子曰：“色难。有事，弟子服其劳；有酒食，先生馔，曾是以为孝乎？”

子夏问孝道。孔子道：“儿子在父母前经常有愉悦的容色，是件难事。有事情，年轻人效劳；有酒有肴，年长的人吃喝，难道这竟可认为是孝么？”

9. 子曰：“吾与回言终日，不违，如愚。退而省其私，亦足以发，回也不愚。”

孔子说：“我整天和颜回讲学，他从不提反对意见和疑问，像个蠢人。等他退回去自己研究，却也能发挥，可见颜回并不愚蠢。”

7. Zi-you asked about being filial. The Master said, "Nowadays for a man to be filial means no more than that he is able to provide his parents with food. Even hounds and horses are, in some way, provided with food. If a man shows no reverence, where is the difference?"

8. Zi-xia asked about being filial. The Master said, "What is difficult to manage is the expression on one's face. As for the young taking on the burden when there is work to be done or letting the old enjoy the wine and the food when these are available, that hardly deserves to be called filial."

9. The Master said, "I can speak to Hui all day without his disagreeing with me in any way.[5] Thus he would seem to be stupid. However, when I take a closer look at what he does in private after he has withdrawn from my presence, I discover that it does, in fact, throw light on what I said. Hui is not stupid after all."

5. Cf. XI.4.

为政篇第二

10. 子曰："视其所以，观其所由，察其所安。人焉廋哉？人焉廋哉？"

孔子说："考查一个人所结交的朋友；观察他为达到一定目的所采用的方式方法；了解他的心情，安于什么，不安于什么。那么，这个人怎样隐藏得住呢？这个人怎样隐藏得住呢？"

11. 子曰："温故而知新，可以为师矣。"

孔子说："在温习旧知识时，能有新体会、新发现，就可以做老师了。"

12. 子曰："君子不器。"

孔子说："君子不像器皿一般，[只有一定的用途。]"

13. 子贡问君子。子曰："先行其言而后从之。"

子贡问怎样才能做一个君子。孔子道："对于你要说的话，先实行了，再说出来[这就够说是一个君子了]。"

14. 子曰："君子周而不比，小人比而不周。"

10. The Master said, "Look at the means a man employs, observe the path he takes and examine where he feels at home.[6] In what way is a man's true character hidden from view? In what way is a man's true character hidden from view?"

6. Cf. "The benevolent man is attracted to benevolence because he feels at home in it." (IV.2)

11. The Master said, "A man is worthy of being a teacher who gets to know what is new by keeping fresh in his mind what he is already familiar with."

12. The Master said, "The gentleman is no vessel. "[7]

7. i.e., he is no specialist, as every vessel is designed for a specific purpose.

13. Zi-gong asked about the gentleman. The Master said, "He puts into effect his words before allowing them to follow the deed."

14. The Master said, "The gentleman enters into associations but not cliques; the small man enters into cliques but not associa-

孔子说："君子是团结，而不是勾结；小人是勾结，而不是团结。"

15. 子曰："学而不思则罔，思而不学则殆。"

孔子说："只是读书，却不思考，就会受骗；只是空想，却不读书，就会缺乏信心。"

16. 子曰："攻乎异端，斯害也已。"

孔子说："批判那些不正确的议论，祸害就可以消灭了。"

17. 子曰："由！诲女知之乎！知之为知之，不知为不知，是知也。"

孔子说："由！教给你对待知或不知的正确态度吧！知道就是知道，不知道就是不知道，这就是聪明智慧。"

18. 子张学干禄。子曰："多闻阙疑，慎言其余，则寡尤；多见阙殆，慎行其余，则寡悔。言寡尤，行寡悔，禄在其中矣。"

子张向孔子学求官职得俸禄的方法。孔子说："多听，有怀疑的地方，加以保留；其余足以自信的部分，谨慎地说出，就能减少错误。多看，有怀疑的地方，加以保留；其余足以

tions."

15. The Master said, "If one learns from others but does not think, one will be bewildered. If, on the other hand, one thinks but does not learn from others, one will be imperilled."

16. The Master said, "To attack a task from the wrong end can do nothing but harm."

17. The Master said, "You, shall I tell you what it is to know. To say you know when you know, and to say you do not when you do not, that is knowledge."

18. Zi-zhang was studying with an eye to an official career. The Master said, "Use your ears widely but leave out what is doubtful; repeat the rest with caution and you will make few mistakes. Use your eyes widely and leave out what is hazardous; put the rest into practice with caution and you will

自信的部分，谨慎地实行，就能减少懊悔。言语的错误少，行动的懊悔少，官职俸禄就在这里面了。”

19. 哀公问曰：“何为则民服？”

孔子对曰：“举直错诸枉，则民服；举枉错诸直，则民不服。”

鲁哀公问道：“要做些什么事才能使百姓服从呢？”

孔子答道：“把正直的人提拔出来，放在邪曲的人之上，百姓就服从了；若是把邪曲的人提拔出来，放在正直的人之上，百姓就会不服从。”

20. 季康子问：“使民敬、忠以劝，如之何？”

子曰：“临之以庄，则敬；孝慈，则忠；举善而教不能，则劝。”

季康子问道：“要使人民严肃认真，尽心竭力和互相勉励，应该怎么办呢？”

孔子说：“你对待人民的事情严肃认真，他们对待你的政令也会严肃认真了；你孝顺父母，慈爱幼小，他们也就会对你尽心竭力了；你提拔好人，教育能力弱的人，他们也就会劝勉了。”

have few regrets. To make few mistakes in speech and to have few regrets in action: therein lies an official career."

19. Duke Ai asked, "What must I do before the common people will look up to me?"

Confucius answered, "Raise the straight and set them over the crooked[8] and the common people will look up to you. Raise the crooked and set them over the straight and the common people will not look up to you."

8. Cf. XII.22.

20. Ji Kang Zi asked, "How can one get the common people to be reverent, to do their utmost and to be filled with enthusiasm?"

The Master said, "Rule over them with dignity and they will be reverent; treat them with kindness and they will do their utmost; raise the good and instruct those who are backward and they will be filled with enthusiasm."

为政篇第二

21. 或谓孔子曰："子奚不为政？"

子曰："《书》云：'孝乎惟孝，友于兄弟，施于有政。'是亦为政，奚其为为政？"

有人对孔子道："你为什么不参与政治？"

孔子道："《尚书》上说：'孝呀，只有孝顺父母，友爱兄弟，把这种风气影响到政治上去。'这也就是参与政治了呀，为什么定要做官才算参与政治呢？"

22. 子曰："人而无信，不知其可也。大车无輗，小车无軏，其何以行之哉？"

孔子说："做为一个人，却不讲信誉，不知那怎么可以。譬如大车子没有安横木的輗，小车子没有安横木的軏，如何能走呢？"

23. 子张问："十世可知也？"

子曰："殷因于夏礼，所损益，可知也；周因于殷礼，所损益，可知也。其或继周者，虽百世，可知也。"

子张问："今后十代［的礼仪制度］可以预先知道吗？"

21. Someone said to Confucius, "Why do you not take part in government?"

The Master said, "The *Book of History* says, 'Oh! Simply by being a good son and friendly to his brothers a man can exert an influence upon government.'[9] In so doing a man is, in fact, taking part in government. How can there be any question of his having actively to 'take part in government'?"

9. This is from a lost chapter of the *Shang Shu* but has been incorporated in a modified form into the spurious *Jun shi* 君奭 chapter.

22. The Master said, "I do not see how a man can be acceptable who is untrustworthy in word. When a pin is missing in the yoke-bar of a large cart or in the collar-bar of a small cart, how can the cart be expected to go?"

23. Zi-zhang asked, "Can ten generations hence be known?"

The Master said, "The Yin built on the rites of the Xia. The additions and the abridgements can be known. The Zhou built on the rites of the Yin. The additions and the abridge-

孔子说："殷朝沿袭夏朝的礼仪制度，所废除的，所增加的，是可以知道的；周朝沿袭殷朝的礼仪制度，所废除的，所增加的，也是可以知道的。那么，假定有继承周朝而当政的人，就是以后一百代，也是可以预先知道的。"

24. 子曰："非其鬼而祭之，谄也。见义不为，无勇也。"

孔子说："不是自己应该祭祀的鬼神，却去祭祀他，这是献媚。眼见应该挺身而出的事情，却袖手旁观，这是怯懦。"

ments can be known. Should there be a successor to the Zhou, even a hundred generations hence can be known."

24. The Master said, "To offer sacrifice to the spirit of an ancestor not one's own is obsequious.

"Seeing what ought to be done, to leave it undone shows a lack of courage."

八佾篇第三

1. 孔子谓季氏，“八佾舞于庭，是可忍也，孰不可忍也？”

孔子谈到季氏，说：“他用六十四人在庭院中奏乐舞蹈，这都可以狠心做出来，什么事不可以狠心做出来呢？”

2. 三家者以《雍》彻。子曰：“‘相维辟公，天子穆穆’，奚取于三家之堂？”

仲孙、叔孙、季孙三家，当他们祭祀祖先时候，［也用天子的礼,］唱着《雍》这篇诗来撤除祭品。孔子说：“［《雍》诗上有这样的话:］‘助祭的是诸侯，天子严肃静穆地在那儿主祭。’这两句话，用在三家祭祖的大厅上在意义上取它哪一点呢？”

3. 子曰：“人而不仁，如礼何？人而不仁，如乐何？”

孔子说：“做了人，却不仁，怎样来对待礼仪制度呢？做了人，却不仁，怎样来对待音乐呢？”

4. 林放问礼之本。子曰：“大哉问！礼，与其奢也，宁俭；丧，与其易也，宁戚。”

林放问礼的本质。孔子说：“你的问题意义重大呀！就一

BOOK 3

1. Confucius said of the Ji family, "They use eight rows of eight dancers each[1] to perform in their courtyard. If this can be tolerated, what cannot be tolerated?"

1. A prerogative of the Emperor.

2. The Three Families[2] performed the *yong*[3] when the sacrificial offerings were being cleared away. The Master said,

"In attendance were the great lords,
In solemn dignity was the Emperor.

What application has this to the halls of the Three Families?"

2. i.e., the three noble families of the state of Lu: Meng–sun 孟孙, Shu–sun 叔孙 and Ji–sun 季孙.

3. Ode 282, from which the couplet quoted comes.

3. The Master said, "What can a man do with the rites who is not benevolent? What can a man do with music who is not benevolent?"

4. Lin Fang asked about the basis of the rites. The Master said, "A noble question indeed! With the rites, it is better to err on the side of frugality than on the side of extravagance; in mourn–

般礼仪说，与其铺张浪费，宁可朴素俭约；就丧礼说，与其仪文周到，宁可过度悲哀。”

5. 子曰：“夷狄之有君，不如诸夏之亡也。”

孔子说：“文化落后国家虽然有个君主，还不如中国没有君主哩。”

6. 季氏旅于泰山。子谓冉有曰：“女弗能救与？”

对曰：“不能。”

子曰：“呜呼！曾谓泰山不如林放乎？”

季氏要去祭祀泰山。孔子对冉有说道：“你不能阻止吗？”

冉有答道：“不能。”

孔子道：“哎呀！竟可以说泰山之神还不及林放［懂礼，居然接受这不合规矩的祭祀］吗？”

7. 子曰：“君子无所争。必也射乎！揖让而升，下而饮。其争也

ing, it is better to err on the side of grief than on the side of indifference."

5. The Master said, "Barbarian tribes with their rulers are inferior to Chinese states without them."

6. The Ji family were going to perform the sacrifice to Mount T'ai.[4] The Master said to Ran You,[5] "Can you not save the situation?"

"No. I cannot."

The Master said, "Alas! Who would have thought that Mount T'ai would suffer in comparison with Lin Fang?"[6]

4. Not being the lord of the state of Lu, the head of the Ji family was not entitled to perform the sacrifice to Mount T'ai and it would be a violation of the rites for Mount T'ai to be offered the sacrifice.
5. who was in the service of the Ji family.
6. See III.4 above where Lin Fang showed a concern for the basis of the rites.

7. The Master said, "There is no contention between gentlemen.

君子。”

孔子说：“君子没有什么可争的事情。如果有所争，一定是比箭吧！[但是当射箭的时候，]相互作揖然后登堂；[射箭完毕，]走下堂来，然后[作揖]喝酒。那一种竞赛是很有礼貌的。”

8. 子夏问曰：“‘巧笑倩兮，美目盼兮，素以为绚兮。’何谓也？”

子曰：“绘事后素。”

曰：“礼后乎？”

子曰：“起予者商也！始可与言《诗》已矣。”

子夏问道：“‘有酒窝的脸笑得美呀，黑白分明的眼流转得媚呀，洁白的底子上画着花卉呀。’这几句诗是什么意思？”

孔子道：“先有白色底子，然后画花。”

子夏道：“那么，是不是礼乐的产生在[仁义]以后呢？”

孔子道：“卜商呀，你真是能启发我的人。现在可以同你讨论《诗经》了。”

9. 子曰：“夏礼，吾能言之，杞不足征也；殷礼，吾能言之，宋

The nearest to it is, perhaps, archery. In archery they bow and make way for one another as they go up and on coming down they drink together. Even the way they contend is gentlemanly."

8. Zi–xia asked,

"Her entrancing smile dimpling,
Her beautiful eyes glancing,
Patterns of colour upon plain silk.[7]

What is the meaning of these lines?"

The Master said, "The plain silk is there first. The colours come afterwards."

"Does the practice of the rites likewise come afterwards?"

The Master said, "It is you, Shang, who have thrown light on the text for me. Only with a man like you can one discuss the *Odes*."

7. The first two lines of this quotation are to be found in Ode 57 but not the third.

9. The Master said, "I am able to discourse on the rites of the

不足征也。文献不足故也。足，则吾能征之矣。”

孔子说：“夏代的礼，我能说出来，它的后代杞国不足以作证；殷代的礼，我能说出来，它的后代宋国不足以作证。这是他们的历史文件和贤者不够的缘故。若有足够的文件和贤者，我就可以引来作证了。”

10. 子曰：“禘自既灌而往者，吾不欲观之矣。”

孔子说：“禘祭的礼，从第一次献酒以后，我就不想看了。”

11. 或问禘之说。子曰：“不知也；知其说者之于天下也，其如示诸斯乎！”指其掌。

Xia, but the state of Qi[8] does not furnish sufficient supporting evidence; I am able to discourse on the rites of the Yin, but the state of Song does not furnish sufficient supporting evidence. This is because there are not enough records and men of erudition. Otherwise I would be able to support what I say with evidence."

8. After the overthrow of the two dynasties, the descendants of the Xia were enfeoffed in the state of Qi while those of the Yin were enfeoffed in the state of Song.

10. The Master said, "I do not wish to witness that part of the *di* sacrifice[9] which follows the opening libation to the impersonator."[10]

9. an important sacrifice performed by the Emperor, but the privilege of performing it was granted to the Duke of Zhou, the founder of the state of Lu.

10. the young boy or girl who impersonates the dead ancestor to whom the offerings are made.

11. Someone asked about the theory of the *di* sacrifice. The Master said, "It is not something I understand, for whoever understands it will be able to manage the Empire as easily as if he

八佾篇第三

有人向孔子请教关于禘祭的理论。孔子说：“我不知道；知道的人对于治理天下，会好像把东西摆在这里一样容易罢！”一面说，一面指着手掌。

12. 祭如在，祭神如神在。子曰：“吾不与祭，如不祭。”

孔子祭祀祖先的时候，便好像祖先真在那里；祭神的时候，便好像神真在那里。孔子又说：“*我若是不能亲自参加祭祀，是不请别人代理的。*”

13. 王孙贾问曰：“与其媚于奥，宁媚于灶，何谓也？”

子曰：“不然；获罪于天，无所祷也。”

王孙贾问道：“‘与其巴结房屋里西南角的神，宁可巴结灶君司命’，这两句话是什么意思？”

孔子道：“不对；若是得罪了上天，祈祷也没用。”

14. 子曰：“周监于二代，郁郁乎文哉！吾从周。”

had it here," pointing to his palm.

12. "Sacrifice as if present" is taken to mean "sacrifice to the gods as if the gods were present."

The Master, however, said, "*Unless I enter into the spirit of a sacrifice, it is as if I did not sacrifice.*"

13. Wang-sun Jia said,

"Better to be obsequious to the kitchen stove

Than to the south-west corner of the house.[11]

What does that mean?"

The Master said, "The saying has got it wrong. When you have offended against Heaven, there is nowhere you can turn to in your prayers."

11. By "the south-west comer of the house", which is the place of honour, Wang-sun Jia, being a minister of Wei, presumably meant to refer to the lord of Wei and by "the kitchen stove" to himself.

14. The Master said, "The Zhou is resplendent in culture, having

孔子说："周朝的礼仪制度是以夏商两代为根据，然后制定的，多么丰富多彩呀！我主张周朝的。"

15. 子入太庙，每事问。或曰："孰谓鄹人之子知礼乎？入太庙，每事问。"

子闻之，曰："是礼也。"

孔子到了周公庙，每件事情都发问。有人便说："谁说叔梁纥的这个儿子懂得礼呢？他到了太庙，每件事都要向别人请教。"

孔子听到了这话，便道："这正是礼呀。"

16. 子曰："射不主皮，为力不同科，古之道也。"

孔子说："比箭，不一定要穿破箭靶子，因为各人的气力大小不一样，这是古时的规矩。"

17. 子贡欲去告朔之饩羊。子曰："赐也！尔爱其羊，我爱其礼。"

before it the example of the two previous dynasties.[12] I am for the Zhou."

12. the Xia and the Yin.

15. When the Master went inside the Grand Temple, [13] he asked questions about everything. Someone remarked, "Who said that the son of the man from Zou[14] understood the rites? When he went inside the Grand Temple, he asked questions about everything."

The Master, on hearing of this, said, "The asking of questions is in itself the correct rite."

13. the temple of the Duke of Zhou, the founder of the state of Lu.

14. The man from Zou refers to Confucius' father.

16. The Master said,

"In archery the point lies not in piercing the hide, [15]
For the reason that strength varies from man to man.

This was the way of antiquity."

15. i.e., the bull's eye fixed in the centre of a cloth target.

17. Zi-gong wanted to do away with the sacrificial sheep at the an-

子贡要把鲁国每月初一告祭祖庙的那只活羊去而不用。孔子道："赐呀！你可惜那只羊，我可惜那种礼。"

18. 子曰："事君尽礼，人以为谄也。"

孔子说："服事君主，一切依照做臣子的礼节做去，别人却以为他在谄媚哩。"

19. 定公问："君使臣，臣事君，如之何？"

孔子对曰："君使臣以礼，臣事君以忠。"

鲁定公问："君主使用臣子，臣子服事君主，各应该怎么样？"

孔子答道："君主应该依礼来使用臣子，臣子应该忠心地服事君主。"

20. 子曰："《关雎》，乐而不淫，哀而不伤。"

孔子说："《关雎》这诗，快乐而不放荡，悲哀而不痛苦。"

21. 哀公问社于宰我。宰我对曰："夏后氏以松，殷人以柏，周人

nouncement of the new moon. The Master said, "Ci, you are loath to part with the price of the sheep, but I am loath to see the disappearance of the rite."

18. The Master said, "You will be looked upon as obsequious by others if you observe every detail of the rites in serving your lord."

19. Duke Ding asked, "How should the ruler employ the services of his subjects? And how should a subject serve his ruler?"

Confucius answered, "The ruler should employ the services of his subjects in accordance with the rites. A subject should serve his ruler by doing his utmost."

20. The Master said, "In the *Guan ju*[16] there is joy but not to the extent of wantonness, and sorrow but not to the extent of self-injury."

16. the first ode in the *Odes*.

21. Duke Ai asked Zai Wo about the altar to the god of earth. Zai

以栗，曰，使民战栗。”

子闻之，曰：“成事不说，遂事不谏，既往不咎。”

鲁哀公向宰我问，作社主用什么木。宰我答道：“夏代用松木，殷代用柏木，周代用栗木，意思是使人民战战栗栗。”

孔子听到了这话，［责备宰我］说：“已经做了的事不便再解释了，已经完成的事不便再挽救了，已经过去的事不便再追究了。”

22. 子曰：“管仲之器小哉！”

或曰：“管仲俭乎？”

曰：“管氏有三归，官事不摄，焉得俭？”

“然则管仲知礼乎？”

曰：“邦君树塞门，管氏亦树塞门。邦君为两君之好，有反坫，管氏亦有反坫。管氏而知礼，孰不知礼？”

孔子说：“管仲的器量狭小得很呀！”

有人便问：“他是不是很节俭呢？”

孔子道：“他收取了人民的大量的市租，他手下的人员，［一人一职，］从不兼差，如何能说是节俭呢？”

那人又问：“那么，他懂得礼节么？”

孔子又道：“国君宫殿门前，立了一个塞门；管氏也立了个塞门；国君设宴招待外国的君主，在堂上有放置酒杯的设

Wo replied, "The Xia used the pine, the Yin used the cedar, and the men of Zhou used the chestnut (*li*), saying that it made the common people tremble (*li*)."

The Master, on hearing of this reply, commented, "One does not explain away what is already done, one does not advise against what is already accomplished, and one does not condemn what has already gone by."

22. The Master said, "Guan Zhong was, indeed, a vessel of small capacity."

Someone remarked, "Was Guan Zhong frugal, then?"

"Guan Zhong kept three establishments, each with a separate staff. How can he be called frugal?"

"In that case, did Guan Zhong understand the rites?"

"Rulers of states erect gate-screens; Guan Zhong erected such a screen as well. The ruler of a state, when entertaining the ruler of another state, has a stand for inverted cups; Guan Zhong had such a stand as well. If even Guan Zhong understood the rites, who does not understand them?"

备，管氏也有这样的设备。假若说他懂得礼节，那谁不懂得礼节呢？”

23. 子语鲁大师乐，曰：“乐其可知也：始作，翕如也；从之，纯如也，皦如也，绎如也，以成。”

孔子把演奏音乐的道理告给鲁国的太师，说道：“音乐，那是可以晓得的：开始演奏，翕翕地热烈；继续下去，纯纯地和谐，皦皦地清晰，绎绎地不绝，这样，然后完成。”

24. 仪封人请见，曰：“君子之至于斯也，吾未尝不得见也。”从者见之。

出曰：“二三子何患于丧乎？天下之无道也久矣，天将以夫子为木铎。”

仪这个地方的边防官请求孔子接见他，说道：“所有到了这个地方的有道德学问的人，我从没有不和他见面的。”

孔子的随行学生请求孔子接见了他。他辞出以后，对孔子的学生们说：“你们这些人为什么着急没有官位呢？天下黑暗日子也长久了，［圣人也该有得意的时候了，］上天会要把他老人家做人民的导师哩。”

25. 子谓《韶》，“尽美矣，又尽善也”。谓《武》，“尽美矣，未

23. The Master talked to the Grand Musician of Lu about music, saying, "This much can be known about music. It begins with playing in unison. When it gets into full swing, it is harmonious, clear and unbroken. In this way it reaches the conclusion."

24. The border official of Yi requested an audience, saying, "I have never been denied an audience by any gentleman who has come to this place." The followers presented him.

When he came out, he said, "What worry have you, gentlemen, about the loss of office? The Empire has long been without the Way. Heaven is about to use your Master as the wooden tongue for a bell." [17]

17. to rouse the Empire.

25. The Master said of the *shao*[18] that it was both perfectly beauti-

尽善也”。

孔子论到《韶》，说：“美极了，而且好极了。”论到《武》，说：“美极了，却还不够好。”

26. 子曰：“居上不宽，为礼不敬，临丧不哀，吾何以观之哉？”

孔子说：“居于统治地位不宽宏大量，行礼的时候不严肃认真，参加丧礼的时候不悲哀，这种样子我怎么看得下去呢？”

ful and perfectly good and of the *wu*[19] that it was perfectly beautiful but not perfectly good.

18. the music of Shun who came to the throne through the abdication of Yao.

19. the music of King Wu who came to the throne through overthrowing the Yin by military force.

26. The Master said, "What can I find worthy of note in a man who is lacking in tolerance when in high position, in reverence when performing the rites and in sorrow when in mourning?"

里仁篇第四

1. 子曰："里仁为美。择不处仁，焉得知？"

孔子说："住的地方，要有仁德这才好。选择住处，没有仁德，怎么能是聪明呢？"

2. 子曰："不仁者不可以久处约，不可以长处乐。仁者安仁，知者利仁。"

孔子说："不仁的人不可以长久地居于穷困中，也不可以长久地居于安乐中。有仁德的人安于仁［实行仁德便心安，不实行仁德心便不安］；聪明人利用仁［他认识到仁德对他长远而巨大的利益，他便实行仁德］。"

3. 子曰："唯仁者能好人，能恶人。"

孔子说："只有仁人才能够喜爱某人，厌恶某人。"

4. 子曰："苟志于仁矣，无恶也。"

孔子说："假如立定志向实行仁德，总没有坏处。"

5. 子曰："富与贵，是人之所欲也；不以其道得之，不处也。贫与贱，是人之所恶也；不以其道得之，不去也。君子去仁，恶乎成名？君子无终食之间违仁，造次必于是，颠沛必于是。"

BOOK 4

1. The Master said, "Of neighbourhoods benevolence is the most beautiful. How can the man be considered wise who, when he has the choice, does not settle in benevolence?"

2. The Master said, "One who is not benevolent cannot remain long in straitened circumstances, nor can he remain long in easy circumstances.

"The benevolent man is attracted to benevolence because he feels at home in it. The wise man is attracted to benevolence because he finds it to his advantage."

3. The Master said, "It is the benevolent man alone who is capable of liking or disliking other men."

4. The Master said, "If a man were to set his heart on benevolence, he would be free from evil."

5. The Master said, "Wealth and high station are what men desire, but unless I got them in the right way I would not abide in them. Poverty and low station are what men dislike, but

里仁篇第四

孔子说："发大财，做大官，这是人人所盼望的；不用正当的方法去得到它，君子不接受。穷困和下贱，这是人人所厌恶的；不用正当的方法去抛掉它，君子不摆脱。君子抛弃了仁德，怎样去成就他的声名呢？君子没有吃完一餐饭的时间离开仁德，就是在仓猝匆忙的时候一定和仁德同在，就是在颠沛流离的时候一定和仁德同在。"

6. 子曰："我未见好仁者，恶不仁者。好仁者，无以尚之；恶不仁者，其为仁矣，不使不仁者加乎其身。有能一日用其力于仁矣乎？我未见力不足者。盖有之矣，我未之见也。"

孔子说："我不曾见到过爱好仁德的人和厌恶不仁德的人。爱好仁德的人，那是再好也没有的了；厌恶不仁德的人，他行仁德，只是不使不仁德的东西加在自己身上。有谁能在某一天使用他的力量于仁德呢？我没见过力量不够的。大概这样的人还是有的，我不曾见到罢了。"

even if I did not get them in the right way I would not try to take myself away from them.[1]

"If the gentleman forsakes benevolence, wherein can he make a name for himself? The gentleman never deserts benevolence, not even for as long as it takes to eat a meal. If he hurries and stumbles one may be sure that it is in benevolence that he does so."

1. This sentence is most likely to be corrupt. The negative is probably an interpolation and the sentence should read: "Poverty and low station are what men dislike, but if I got them in the right way I would not try to take myself away from them."

6. The Master said, "I have never met a man who finds benevolence attractive or a man who finds unbenevolence[2] repulsive. A man who finds benevolence attractive cannot be surpassed. A man who finds unbenevolence repulsive can, perhaps, be counted as benevolent, for he would not allow what is not benevolent to be inflicted on his person.

"Is there a man who, for the space of a single day, is able to devote all his strength to benevolence? I have not come across such a man whose strength proves insufficient for the task.

7. 子曰："人之过也，各于其党。观过，斯知仁矣。"

孔子说："[人是各种各样的，人的错误也是各种各样的。]什么样的错误就是由什么样的人犯的。仔细考察某人所犯的错误，就可以知道他是什么样式的人了。"

8. 子曰："朝闻道，夕死可矣。"

孔子说："早晨得知真理，要我当晚死去，都可以。"

9. 子曰："士志于道，而耻恶衣恶食者，未足与议也。"

孔子说："读书人有志于真理，但又以自己吃粗粮穿破衣为耻辱，这种人，不值得同他商议了。"

There must be such cases of insufficient strength, only I have not come across them."[3]

2. The word "unbenevolence" has been coined because the original word does not simply mean the absence of benevolence as "nonbenevolence" would convey but something positive as, for instance, in a word like "unkind".

3. Cf. VI.12.

7. The Master said, "In his errors a man is true to type. Observe the errors and you will know the man."

8. The Master said, "He has not lived in vain who dies in the evening, having been told about the Way in the morning."

9. The Master said, "There is no point in seeking the views of a Gentleman[4] who, though he sets his heart on the Way, is ashamed of poor food and poor clothes."

4. Throughout this book, "Gentleman" is used as a equivalent for *shi* 士 while "gentleman" is used for *jun zi* 君子.

里仁篇第四

10. 子曰："君子之于天下也，无适也，无莫也，义之与比。"

孔子说："君子对于天下的事情，没规定要怎样干，也没规定不要怎样干，只要怎样干合理恰当，便怎样干。"

11. 子曰："君子怀德，小人怀土；君子怀刑，小人怀惠。"

孔子说："君子怀念道德，小人怀念乡土；君子关心法度，小人关心恩惠。"

12. 子曰："放于利而行，多怨。"

孔子说："依据个人利益而行动，会招致很多的怨恨。"

13. 子曰："能以礼让为国乎？何有？不能以礼让为国，如礼何？"

孔子说："能够用礼让来治理国家吗？这有什么困难呢？如果不能用礼让来治理国家，又怎样来对待礼仪呢？"

10. The Master said, "In his dealings with the world the gentleman is not invariably for or against anything. He is on the side of what is moral."

11. The Master said, "While the gentleman cherishes benign rule, the small man cherishes his native land. While the gentleman cherishes a respect for the law, the small man cherishes generous treatment." [5]

5. The distinction here between "the gentleman" and "the small man" is not, as is often the case, drawn between the ruler and the ruled but within the class of the ruled.

12. The Master said, "If one is guided by profit in one's actions, one will incur much ill will."

13. The Master said, "For a man who is able to govern a state by observing the rites and showing deference, what is there to holding office? For a man who is unable to govern a state by observing the rites and showing deference, what good can the rites be to him?"

14. 子曰："不患无位，患所以立。不患莫己知，求为可知也。"

孔子说："不发愁没有职位，只发愁没有任职的本领；不怕没有人知道自己，去追求足以使别人知道自己的本领好了。"

15. 子曰："参乎！吾道一以贯之。"

曾子曰："唯。"

子出，门人问曰："何谓也？"

曾子曰："夫子之道，忠恕而已矣。"

孔子说："参呀！我的学说贯穿着一个基本观念。"

曾子说："是。"

孔子走出去以后，别的学生便问曾子道："这是什么意思？"

曾子道："他老人家的学说，只是忠和恕罢了。"

16. 子曰："君子喻于义，小人喻于利。"

孔子说："君子懂得的是义，小人懂得的是利。"

17. 子曰："见贤思齐焉，见不贤而内自省也。"

孔子说："看见贤人，便应该想向他看齐；看见不贤的人，

14. The Master said, "Do not worry about your lack of official position. Worry about what would earn you a position. Do not worry about the lack of appreciation of your abilities on the part of others. Seek to be worthy of appreciation."

15. The Master said, "Shen! There is one single thread binding my way together."[6]

Zeng Zi assented.

After the Master had gone out, the disciples asked, "What did he mean?"

Zeng Zi said, "The way of the Master consists in doing one's best and in using oneself as a measure to gauge the likes and dislikes of others. That is all."

6. Cf. XV.3.

16. The Master said, "The gentleman is versed in what is moral. The small man is versed in what is profitable."

17. The Master said, "When you meet someone better than yourself, turn your thoughts to becoming his equal. When you meet

便应该自己反省，［有没有同他类似的毛病。］”

18. 子曰："事父母几谏，见志不从，又敬不违，劳而不怨。"

孔子说："侍奉父母，［如果他们有不对的地方，］得轻微婉转地劝止，看到自己的心意没有被听从，仍然恭敬地不触犯他们，虽然忧愁，但不怨恨。"

19. 子曰："父母在，不远游，游必有方。"

孔子说："父母在世，不出远门，如果要出远门，必须有一定的去处。"

20. 子曰："三年无改于父之道，可谓孝矣。"

孔子说："若是他对他父亲的合理部分，长期地不加改变，可以说做到孝了。"

21. 子曰："父母之年，不可不知也。一则以喜，一则以惧。"

孔子说："父母的年纪不能不时时记在心里:一方面因［其高寿］而喜欢，另一方面又因［其寿高］而有所恐惧。"

someone not as good as you are, look within and examine your own self."

18. The Master said, "In serving your father and mother you ought to dissuade them from doing wrong in the gentlest way. If you see your advice being ignored, you should not become disobedient but should remain reverent. You should not complain even if you are distressed."

19. The Master said, "While your parents are alive, you should not travel too far afield. If you do travel, your whereabouts should always be known."

20. The Master said, "If, for three years, a man makes no changes to his father's ways, he can be said to be a good son."[7]

7. This saying also forms part of I. 11.

21. The Master said," A man should not be unaware of the age of his father and mother. It is a matter, on the one hand, for rejoicing and, on the other, for anxiety."

里仁篇第四

22. 子曰："古者言之不出，耻躬之不逮也。"

孔子说："古时候言语不轻易出口，就是怕自己的行动赶不上。"

23. 子曰："以约失之者鲜矣。"

孔子说："因为对自己节制、约束而犯过失的，这种事情总不会多。"

24. 子曰："君子欲讷于言而敏于行。"

孔子说："君子言语要谨慎迟钝，工作要勤劳敏捷。"

25. 子曰："德不孤，必有邻。"

孔子说："有道德的人不会孤单，一定会有［志同道合的人来和他做］伙伴。"

26. 子游曰："事君数，斯辱矣；朋友数，斯疏矣。"

子游说："对待君主过于烦琐，就会招致侮辱；对待朋友过于烦琐，就会反被疏远。"

BOOK 4

22. The Master said, "In antiquity men were loath to let their words issue forth. This was because they counted it shameful if their persons failed to keep up with their words."

23. The Master said, "It is rare for a man to miss the mark through keeping to essentials."[8]

8. Cf. "He [i.e., the Master] broadens me with culture and brings me back to essentials by means of the rites." (IX. 11)

24. The Master said, "It is desirable for a gentleman to be slow of speech but quick in action."

25. The Master said, "Virtue never stands alone. It is bound to have neighbours."

26. Zi-you said, "To be importunate with one's lord will mean humiliation. To be importunate with one's friends will mean estrangement."

公冶长篇第五

1. 子谓公冶长，“可妻也。虽在缧绁之中，非其罪也”。以其子妻之。

孔子说公冶长，“可以把女儿嫁给他。他虽然曾被关在监狱之中，但不是他的罪过”。便把自己的女儿嫁给他。

2. 子谓南容，“邦有道，不废；邦无道，免于刑戮”。以其兄之子妻之。

孔子说南容，“国家政治清明，［总有官做，］不被废弃；国家政治黑暗，也不致被刑罚”。于是把自己的侄女嫁给他。

3. 子谓子贱，“君子哉若人！鲁无君子者，斯焉取斯？”

孔子评论宓子贱，说：“这人是君子呀！假若鲁国没有君子，这种人从哪里取来这种好品德呢？”

4. 子贡问曰：“赐也何如？”

子曰：“女，器也。”

曰：“何器也？”

曰：“瑚琏也。”

子贡问道：“我是一个怎样的人？”

孔子道：“你好比是一个器皿。”

BOOK 5

1. The Master said of Gong-ye Chang that he was a suitable choice for a husband, for though he was in gaol it was not through any wrongdoing on his part. He gave him his daughter in marriage.

2. The Master said of Nan-rong that when the Way prevailed in the state he was not cast aside and when the Way fell into disuse he stayed clear of the humiliation of punishment. He gave him his elder brother's daughter in marriage. [1]

1. Cf. XI.6.

3. The Master's comment on Zi-jian was "What a gentleman this man is! If there were no gentlemen in Lu where could he have taken his qualities from?"

4. Zi-gong asked, "What do you think of me?"

The Master said, "You are a vessel."[2]

"What kind of vessel?"

"A sacrificial vessel."[3]

2. Cf. II.13.

3. made of jade.

公冶长篇第五

子贡道："什么器皿？"

孔子道："宗庙里盛黍稷的瑚琏。"

5. 或曰："雍也仁而不佞。"

子曰："焉用佞？御人以口给，屡憎于人。不知其仁，焉用佞？"

有人说："冉雍这个人有仁德，却没有口才。"

孔子道："何必要口才呢？强嘴利舌地同人家辩驳，常常被人讨厌。冉雍未必仁，但为什么要有口才呢？"

6. 子使漆雕开仕。对曰："吾斯之未能信。"子说。

孔子叫漆雕开去做官。他答道："我对这个还没有信心。"孔子听了很欢喜。

7. 子曰："道不行，乘桴浮于海。从我者，其由与？"子路闻之喜。子曰："由也好勇过我，无所取材。"

孔子道："主张行不通了，我想坐个木簰到海外去，跟随我的恐怕只有仲由吧！"子路听到这话，高兴得很。孔子说："仲由这个人太好勇敢了，好勇的精神大大超过了我，这就没有什么可取的呀！"

BOOK 5

5. Someone said, "Yong is benevolent but does not have a facile tongue."

The Master said, "What need is there for a facile tongue? A man quick with a retort will frequently incur the hatred of others. I can not say whether Yong is benevolent or not, but what need is there for a facile tongue?"

6. The Master told Qi-diao Kai to take office. Qi-diao Kai said, "I cannot trust myself to do so yet." The Master was pleased.

7. The Master said, "Should the Way fail to prevail and I were to put to sea on a raft, the one to follow me would, I suppose, be You." Zi-lu, on hearing this, was overjoyed. The Master said, "You is more foolhardy than I. *He has not even a supply of timber for his raft.*"

公冶长篇第五

8. 孟武伯问子路仁乎？子曰："不知也。"又问。子曰："由也，千乘之国，可使治其赋也，不知其仁也。"

"求也何如？"

子曰："求也，千室之邑，百乘之家，可使为之宰也，不知其仁也。"

"赤也何如？"

子曰："赤也，束带立于朝，可使与宾客言也，不知其仁也。"

孟武伯向孔子问子路有没有仁德。孔子道："不晓得。"他又问。孔子道："仲由啦，如果有一千辆兵车的国家，可以叫他负责兵役和军政的工作。至于他有没有仁德，我不晓得。"

孟武伯继续问："冉求又怎么样呢？"

孔子道："求啦，千户人口的私邑，可以叫他当县长；百辆兵车的大夫封地，可以叫他当总管。至于他有没有仁德，我不晓得。"

"公西赤又怎么样呢？"

孔子道："赤啦，穿着礼服，立于朝廷之中，可以叫他接待外宾，办理交涉。至于他有没有仁德，我不晓得。"

9. 子谓子贡曰："女与回也孰愈？"

对曰："赐也何敢望回？回也闻一以知十，赐也闻一以知

BOOK 5

8. Meng Wu Bo asked whether Zi–lu was benevolent. The Master said, "I cannot say." Meng Wu Bo repeated the question. The Master said, "You can be given the responsibility of managing the military levies in a state of a thousand chariots, but whether he is benevolent or not I cannot say."

"What about Qiu?"

The Master said, "Qiu can be given the responsibility of a steward in a town with a thousand households or in a noble family with a hundred chariots, but whether he is benevolent or not I can not say."

"What about Chi?"

The Master said, "When Chi takes his place at court, wearing his sash, he can be given the responsibility of conversing with the guests, but whether he is benevolent or not I cannot say."

9. The Master said to Zi–gong, "Who is the better man, you or Hui?"

二。”

子曰：“弗如也；吾与女弗如也。”

孔子对子贡道：“你和颜回，哪一个强些？”

子贡答道：“我么，怎敢和回相比？他啦，听到一件事，可以推演知道十件事；我咧，听到一件事，只能推知两件事。”

孔子道：“赶不上他；*我同意你的话，是*赶不上他。”

10. 宰予昼寝。子曰：“朽木不可雕也，粪土之墙不可杇也；于予与何诛？”子曰：“始吾于人也，听其言而信其行；今吾于人也，听其言而观其行。于予与改是。”

宰予在白天睡觉。孔子说：“腐烂了的木头雕刻不得，粪土似的墙壁粉刷不得；对于宰予么，不值得责备呀。”又说：“最初，我对人家，听到他的话，便相信他的行为；今天，我对人家，听到他的话，却要考察他的行为。从宰予的事件以后，我改变了态度。”

11. 子曰：“吾未见刚者。”

或对曰：“申枨。”

子曰：“枨也欲，焉得刚？”

孔子道：“我没见过刚毅不屈的人。”

"How dare I compare myself with Hui? When he is told one thing he understands ten. When I am told one thing I understand only two."

The Master said, "You are not as good as he is. *Neither of us is as good as he is.*"

10. Zai Yu was in bed in the daytime. The Master said, "A piece of rotten wood cannot be carved, nor can a wall of dried dung be trowelled. As far as Yu is concerned what is the point in condemning him.?" The Master added, "I used to take on trust a man's deeds after having listened to his words. Now having listened to a man's words I go on to observe his deeds. It was on account of Yu that I have changed in this respect."

11. The Master said, "I have never met anyone who is truly unbending."

Someone said, "What about Shen Cheng?"

The Master said, "Cheng is full of desires. How can he be

有人答道："申枨是这样的人。"

孔子道："申枨啦，他欲望太多，哪里能够刚毅不屈？"

12. 子贡曰："我不欲人之加诸我也，吾亦欲无加诸人。"

子曰："赐也，非尔所及也。"

子贡道："我不想别人欺侮我，我也不想欺侮别人。"

孔子说："赐，这不是你能做到的。"

13. 子贡曰："夫子之文章，可得而闻也；夫子之言性与天道，不可得而闻也。"

子贡说："老师关于文献方面的学问，我们听得到；老师关于天性和天道的言论，我们听不到。"

14. 子路有闻，未之能行，唯恐有闻。

子路有所闻，还没有能够去做，只怕又有所闻。

15. 子贡问曰："孔文子何以谓之'文'也？"

子曰："敏而好学，不耻下问，是以谓之'文'也。"

子贡问道："孔文子凭什么谥他为'文'？"

孔子道："他聪敏灵活，爱好学问，又谦虚下问，不以为

unbending?"

12. Zi-gong said, "While I do not wish others to impose on me, I wish not to impose on others either."

The Master said, "Ci, that is quite beyond you."

13. Zi-gong said, "One can get to hear about the Master's accomplishments, but one cannot get to hear his views on human nature and the Way of Heaven."

14. Before he could put into practice something he had heard, the only thing Zi-lu feared was that he should be told something further.

15. Zi-gong asked, "Why was Kun Wen Zi called 'wen'?"

The Master said, "He was quick and eager to learn: he was not ashamed to seek the advice of those who were beneath him in station. That is why he was called 'wen'."[4]

耻，所以用‘文’字做他的谥号。”

16. 子谓子产有君子之道四焉：其行己也恭，其事上也敬，其养民也惠，其使民也义。

孔子评论子产，说他有四种行为合于君子之道：他自己的容颜态度庄严恭敬，他对待君上负责认真，他教养人民有恩惠，他役使人民合于道理。

17. 子曰："晏平仲善与人交，久而敬之。"

孔子说："晏平仲善于和别人交朋友，相交越久，别人越发恭敬他。"

18. 子曰："臧文仲居蔡，山节藻棁，何如其知也？"

孔子说："臧文仲替一种叫蔡的大乌龟盖了一间屋，有雕刻着像山一样的斗栱和画着藻草的梁上短柱，这个人的聪明怎么这样呢？"

4. In the chapter dealing with posthumous titles in the *Yi Zhou shu* 逸周书 it is said that "diligence in learning and seeking advice is called 'wen'" (p. 196). It is likely that the *Yi Zhou shu*, though traditionally taken to be earlier, in fact took the Analects as one of its sources.

16. The Master said of Zi-chan that he had the way of the gentleman on four counts: he was respectful in the manner he conducted himself; he was reverent in the service of his lord; in caring for the common people, he was generous and, in employing their services, he was just.

17. The Master said, "Yan Ping-zhong excels in being friends with others: Even after long acquaintance his reverence does not flag."

18. The Master said, "When housing his giant tortoise,[5] Zang Wen-zhong had the capitals of the pillars carved in the shape of hills and the rafterposts painted in a duckweed design. What is one to think of his intelligence?"

5. whose shell is used for divination.

19. 子张问曰："令尹子文三仕为令尹，无喜色；三已之，无愠色。旧令尹之政，必以告新令尹。何如？"

子曰："忠矣。"

曰："仁矣乎？"

曰："未知；——焉得仁？"

"崔子弑齐君，陈文子有马十乘，弃而违之。至于他邦，则曰：'犹吾大夫崔子也。'违之。之一邦，则又曰：'犹吾大夫崔子也。'违之。何如？"

子曰："清矣。"

曰："仁矣乎？"

曰："未知；——焉得仁？"

子张问道："楚国的令尹子文三次做令尹的官，没有高兴的颜色；三次被罢免，没有怨恨的颜色。[每次交代，] 一定把自己的一切政令全部告诉接位的人。这个人怎么样？"

孔子道："可算尽忠于国家了。"

子张道："算不算仁呢？"

孔子道："不晓得；——这怎么能算是仁呢？"

子张又问："崔杼无理地杀掉齐庄公，陈文子有四十匹马，舍弃不要，离开齐国。到了另一个国家，说道：'这里的执政者同我们的崔子差不多。'又离开。又到了一国，又说道：'这里的执政者同我们的崔子差不多。'于是又离开。这个人怎么

19. Zi-zhang asked, "Ling Yin[6] Zi-wen gave no appearance of pleasure when he was made prime minister three times. Neither did he give any appearance of displeasure when he was removed from office three times. He always told his successor what he had done during his term of office. What do you think of this?"

The Master said, "He can, indeed, be said to be a man who does his best."

"Can he be said to be benevolent?"

"*He cannot even be said to be wise*. How can he be said to be benevolent?"

"When Cui Zi assassinated the Lord of Qi, Chen Wen Zi who owned ten teams of four horses each abandoned them and left the state. On arriving in another state, he said, 'The officials here are no better than our Counsellor Cui Zi.' He left and went to yet another state. Once more, he said, 'The officials here are no better than our Counsellor Cui Zi,' and he again left. What do you think of this?"

The Master said, "He can, indeed, be said to be pure."

"Can he be said to be benevolent?"

"*He cannot even be said to be wise*. How can he be said to

样？”

孔子道：“清白得很。”

子张道：“算不算仁呢？”

孔子道：“不晓得；——这怎么能算是仁呢？”

20. 季文子三思而后行。子闻之，曰：“再，斯可矣。”

季文子每件事考虑多次才行动。孔子听到了，说：“想两次也就可以了。”

21. 子曰：“宁武子，邦有道，则知；邦无道，则愚。其知可及也，其愚不可及也。”

孔子说：“宁武子在国家太平时节，便聪明；在国家昏暗时节，便装傻。他那聪明，别人赶得上；那装傻，别人就赶不上了。”

22. 子在陈，曰：“归与！归与！吾党之小子狂简，斐然成章，不知所以裁之。”

孔子在陈国，说：“回去吧！回去吧！我们那里的学生们志向高大得很，文彩又都斐然可观，我不知道怎样去指导他们。”

be benevolent?"

6. This was the title in the state of Chu for the prime minister.

20. Ji Wen Zi always thought three times before taking action. When the Master was told of this, he commented, "Twice is quite enough."

21. The Master said, "Ning Wu Zi was intelligent when the Way prevailed in the state, but stupid when it did not. His intelligence was within reach of others, but not his stupidity."

22. When he was in Chen, the Master said, "Let us go home. Let us go home. Our young men at home are wildly ambitious, and have great accomplishments for all to see, *but they do not know how to prune themselves.*"[7]

7. Cf. Mencius, VII.B.37.

公冶长篇第五

23. 子曰："伯夷、叔齐不念旧恶，怨是用希。"

孔子说："伯夷、叔齐这两兄弟不记念过去的仇恨，别人对他们的怨恨也就很少。"

24. 子曰："孰谓微生高直？或乞醯焉，乞诸其邻而与之。"

孔子说："谁说微生高这个人直爽？有人向他讨点醋，[他不说自己没有，]却到邻人那里转讨一点给人。"

25. 子曰："巧言、令色、足恭，左丘明耻之，丘亦耻之。匿怨而友其人，左丘明耻之，丘亦耻之。"

孔子说："花言巧语，伪善的容貌，十足的恭顺，这种态度，左丘明认为可耻，我也认为可耻。内心藏着怨恨，表面上却同他要好，这种行为，左丘明认为可耻，我也认为可耻。"

26. 颜渊季路侍。子曰："盍各言尔志？"

子路曰："愿车马衣轻裘与朋友共敝之而无憾。"

颜渊曰："愿无伐善，无施劳。"

子路曰："愿闻子之志。"

子曰："老者安之，朋友信之，少者怀之。"

23. The Master said, "Bo Yi and Shu Qi never remembered old scores. For this reason they rarely incurred ill will."

24. The Master said, "Who said Wei-sheng Gao was straight? Once when someone begged him for vinegar, he went and begged it off a neighbour to give it to him."

25. The Master said, "Cunning words, an ingratiating countenance and utter servility, these things Zuo-qiu Ming found shameful. I, too, find them shameful. To be friendly towards someone while concealing a sense of grievance, this Zuo-qiu Ming found shameful. I, too, find it shameful."

26. Yan Yuan and Ji-lu were in attendance. The Master said, "Why do you not each tell me what it is you have set your hearts on."

Zi-lu said, "I should like to share my carriage and horses, clothes and furs with my friends, and to have no regrets even if

孔子坐着，颜渊、季路两人站在孔子身边。孔子道：“何不各人说说自己的志向？”

子路道：“愿意把我的车马衣服同朋友共同使用坏了也没有什么不满。”

颜渊道：“愿意不夸耀自己的好处，不表白自己的功劳。”

子路向孔子道：“希望听到您的志向。”

孔子道：“[我的志向是，]老者使他安逸，朋友使他信任我，年轻人使他怀念我。”

27. 子曰：“已矣乎，吾未见能见其过而内自讼者也。”

孔子说：“算了吧！我没有看见过能够看到自己的错误便自我责备的哩。”

28. 子曰：“十室之邑，必有忠信如丘者焉，不如丘之好学也。”

孔子说：“就是十户人家的地方，一定有像我这样又忠心又信实的人，只是赶不上我的喜欢学问罢了。”

they become worn."

Yan Yuan said, "I should like never to boast of my own goodness and never to impose onerous tasks upon others."

Zi–lu said, "I should like to hear what you have set your heart on."

The Master said, "To bring peace to the old, to have trust in my friends, and to cherish the young."

27. The Master said, "I suppose I should give up hope. I have yet to meet the man who, on seeing his own errors, is able to take himself to task inwardly."[8]

8. Cf. IV.17.

28. The Master said, "In a hamlet of ten households, there are bound to be those who are my equal in doing their best for others and in being trustworthy in what they say, but they are unlikely to be as eager to learn as I am."

雍也篇第六

1. 子曰："雍也可使南面。"

孔子说："冉雍这个人，可以让他做一部门或一地方的长官。"

2. 仲弓问子桑伯子。子曰："可也简。"

仲弓曰："居敬而行简，以临其民，不亦可乎？居简而行简，无乃大简乎？"

子曰："雍之言然。"

仲弓问到子桑伯子这个人。孔子道："他简单得好。"

仲弓道："若存心严肃认真，而以简单行之，[抓大体，不烦琐，]来治理百姓，不也可以吗？若存心简单，又以简单行之，不是太简单了吗？"

孔子道："你这番话正确。"

3. 哀公问："弟子孰为好学？"

孔子对曰："有颜回者好学，不迁怒，不贰过。不幸短命死矣，今也则亡，未闻好学者也。"

鲁哀公问："你的学生中，哪个好学？"

孔子答道："有一个叫颜回的人好学，不拿别人出气；也不再犯同样的过失。不幸短命死了，现在再没有这样的人了，再也没听过好学的人了。"

BOOK 6

1. The Master said, "Yong could be given the seat facing south."[1]

1. the seat of the ruler.

2. Zhong–gong asked about Zi–sang Bo–zi. The Master said, "It is his simplicity of style that makes him acceptable."

Zhong–gong said, "In ruling over the common people, is it not acceptable to hold oneself in reverence and merely to be simple in the measures one takes? On the other hand, is it not carrying simplicity too far to be simple in the way one holds oneself as well as in the measures one takes?"

The Master said, "Yong is right in what he says."

3. Duke Ai asked which of his disciples was eager to learn.

Confucius answered, "There was one Yan Hui who was eager to learn. He never transferred the anger he felt towards one person to another. Nor did he make the same mistake twice. Unfortunately his allotted span was a short one and he died. Now there is no one. No one eager to learn has come to my notice."

4. 子华使于齐，冉子为其母请粟。子曰："与之釜。"请益。曰："与之庾。"冉子与之粟五秉。

子曰："赤之适齐也，乘肥马，衣轻裘。吾闻之也:君子周急不继富。"

公西华被派到齐国去作使者，冉有替他母亲向孔子请求小米。孔子道："给他六斗四升。"冉有请求增加。孔子道："再给他二斗四升。"冉有却给了他八十石。

孔子道："公西赤到齐国去，坐着由肥马驾的车辆，穿着又轻又暖的皮袍。我听说过:君子只是雪里送炭，不去锦上添花。"

5. 原思为之宰，与之粟九百，辞。子曰："毋！以与尔邻里乡党乎!"

原思任孔子家的总管，孔子给他小米九百，他不肯受。孔子道："别辞！有多的，给你地方上［的穷人］吧!"

6. 子谓仲弓，曰："犁牛之子骍且角，虽欲勿用，山川其舍诸?"

孔子谈到冉雍，说："耕牛的儿子长着赤色的毛，整齐的角，虽然不想用它作牺牲来祭祀，山川之神难道会舍弃它吗?"

BOOK 6

4. Ran Zi asked for grain for the mother of Zi–hua who was away on a mission to Qi. The Master said, "Give her one *fu*."[2] Ran Zi asked for more. "Give her one *yu*." Ran Zi gave her five *bing* of grain.

The Master said, "Chi went off to Qi in a carriage drawn by well–fed horses and was wearing light furs. I have heard it said, 'A gentleman gives to help the needy and not to maintain the rich in style.'"

2. *Fu*, *yu* and *bing* are dry measures in ascending order of capacity.

5. On becoming his[3] steward, Yuan Si was given nine hundred measures of grain which he declined. The Master said, "Can you not find a use for it in helping the people in your neigh–bourhood?"

3. i.e., Confucius'.

6. The Master said of Zhong–gong, "Should a bull born of plough cattle have a sorrel coat and well–formed horns, would the spirits of the mountains and rivers allow it to be passed over even if we felt it was not good enough to be used?"

雍也篇第六

7. 子曰："回也，其心三月不违仁，其余则日月至焉而已矣。"

孔子说："颜回呀，他的心长久地不离开仁德，别的学生么，只是短时期偶然想起一下罢了。"

8. 季康子问："仲由可使从政也与？"

子曰："由也果，于从政乎何有？"

曰："赐也可使从政也与？"

曰："赐也达，于从政乎何有？"

曰："求也可使从政也与？"

曰："求也艺，于从政乎何有？"

季康子问孔子："仲由这人，可以使用他治理政事么？"

孔子道："仲由果敢决断，让他治理政事有什么困难呢？"

又问："端木赐可以使用他治理政事么？"

孔子道："端木赐通情达理，让他治理政事有什么困难呢？"

又问："冉求可以使用他治理政事么？"

孔子道："冉求多才多艺，让他治理政事有什么困难呢？"

9. 季氏使闵子骞为费宰。闵子骞曰："善为我辞焉！如有复我者，则吾必在汶上矣。"

季氏叫闵子骞作他采邑费地的县长。闵子骞对来人说道：

7. The Master said, "For three months at a time Hui does not lapse from benevolence in his heart. The others attain benevolence merely by fits and starts."

8. Ji Kang Zi asked, "Is zhong You good enough to be given office?"

The Master said, "You is resolute. What is there to taking office for him?"

"Is Ci good enough to be given office?"

"Ci is a man of understanding. What is there to taking office for him?"

"Is Qiu good enough to be given office?"

"Qiu is accomplished. What is there to taking office for him?"

9. The Ji family wanted to make Min Zi–qian the steward of Bi. Min Zi–qian said, "Decline the offer for me tactfully. If anyone comes back for me, I shall be on the other side of the

"好好地替我辞掉吧！若是再来找我的话，那我一定会逃到汶水之北去了。"

10. 伯牛有疾，子问之，自牖执其手，曰："亡之，命矣夫！斯人也而有斯疾也！斯人也而有斯疾也！"

伯牛生了病，孔子去探问他，从窗户里握着他的手，道："难得活了，这是命呀！这样的人竟有这样的病！这样的人竟有这样的病！"

11. 子曰："贤哉，回也！一箪食，一瓢饮，在陋巷，人不堪其忧，回也不改其乐。贤哉，回也！"

孔子说："颜回多么有修养呀！一竹筐饭，一瓜瓢水，住在小巷子里，别人都受不了那穷苦的忧愁，颜回却不改变他自有的快乐。颜回多么有修养呀！"

12. 冉求曰："非不说子之道，力不足也。"

子曰："力不足者，中道而废。今女画。"

冉求道："不是我不喜欢您的学说，是我力量不够。"孔子道："如果真是力量不够，走到半道会再走不动了。现在你却没有开步走。"

River Wen."[4]

4. i.e., over the border into the state of Qi.

10. Bo–niu was ill. The Master visited him and, holding his hand through the window, said, "We are going to lose him. It must be Destiny. Why else should such a man be stricken with such a disease? Why else should such a man be stricken with such a disease?"

11. The Master said, "How admirable Hui is! Living in a mean dwelling on a bowlful of rice and a ladleful of water is a hardship most men would find insupportable, but Hui does not allow this to affect his joy. How admirable Hui is!"

12. Ran Qiu said, "It is not that I am not pleased with your way, but rather that my strength gives out."

The Master said, "A man whose strength gives out collapses along the course. *In your case you set the limits beforehand.*"

雍也篇第六

13. 子谓子夏曰："女为君子儒！无为小人儒！"

孔子对子夏道："你要去做个君子式的儒者，不要去做那小人式的儒者！"

14. 子游为武城宰。子曰："女得人焉耳乎？"

曰："有澹台灭明者，行不由径，非公事，未尝至于偃之室也。"

子游做武城县县长。孔子道："你在这儿得到什么人才没有？"

他道："有一个叫澹台灭明的人，走路不插小道，不是公事，从不到我屋里来。"

15. 子曰："孟之反不伐，奔而殿，将入门，策其马，曰：'非敢后也，马不进也。'"

孔子说："孟之反不夸耀自己，［在抵御齐国的战役中，右翼的军队溃退了，］他走在最后，掩护全军，将进城门，便鞭打着马匹，一面说道：'不是我敢于殿后，是马匹不肯快走的缘故。'"

13. The Master said to Zi-xia, "Be a gentleman *ru*, [5] not a petty *ru*."

5. The original meaning of the word is uncertain, but it probably referred to men for whom the qualities of the scholar were more important than those of the warrior. In subsequent ages, *ru* came to be the name given to the Confucianists.

14. Zi-you was the steward of Wu Cheng. The Master said, "Have you discovered any exceptional people there?"

"There is one Dan-tai Mie-ming who never takes short cuts and who has never been to my room except on official business."

15. The Master said, "Meng Zhi Fan was not given to boasting. When the army was routed, he brought up the rear. But on entering the gate, he goaded his horse on, saying, 'It was not that I dared lag behind, but my horse simply refused to advance.'"

雍也篇第六

16. 子曰：“不有祝鮀之佞，而有宋朝之美，难乎免于今之世矣。”

孔子说：“假使没有祝鮀的口才，而仅有宋朝的美丽，在今天的社会里怕不易避免祸害了。”

17. 子曰：“谁能出不由户？何莫由斯道也？”

孔子说：“谁能够走出屋外不从房门经过？为什么没有人从我这条路行走呢？”

18. 子曰：“质胜文则野，文胜质则史。文质彬彬，然后君子。”

孔子说：“朴实多于文采，就未免粗野；文采多于朴实，又未免虚浮。文采和朴实，配合适当，这才是个君子。”

19. 子曰：“人之生也直，罔之生也幸而免。”

孔子说：“人的生存由于正直，不正直的人也可以生存，那是他侥幸地免于祸害。”

20. 子曰：“知之者不如好之者，好之者不如乐之者。”

16. The Master said, "You may have the good looks of Song Chao, but you will find it difficult to escape unscathed in this world if you do not, at the same time, have the smooth tongue of the Priest Tuo."

17. The Master said, "Who can go out without using the door? Why, then, does no one follow this Way?"

18. The Master said, "When there is a preponderance of native substance over acquired refinement, the result will be churlishness. When there is a preponderance of acquired refinement over native substance, the result will be pedantry. Only a well-balanced admixture of the two will result in gentlemanliness."

19. The Master said, "That a man lives is because he is straight. That a man who dupes others survives is because he has been fortunate enough to be spared."

20. The Master said, "To be fond of it is better than merely to know it, and to find joy in it is better than merely to be fond

孔子说："[对于任何学问和事业，] 懂得它的人不如喜爱它的人，喜爱它的人又不如以它为乐的人。"

21. 子曰："中人以上，可以语上也；中人以下，不可以语上也。"

孔子说："中等水平以上的人，可以告诉他高深学问；中等水平以下的人，不可以告诉他高深学问。"

22. 樊迟问知。子曰："务民之义，敬鬼神而远之，可谓知矣。"

问仁。曰："仁者先难而后获，可谓仁矣。"

樊迟问怎么样才算聪明。孔子道："把心力专一地放在使人民走向'义'上，严肃地对待鬼神，但并不打算接近他，可以说是聪明了。"

又问怎么样才叫做有仁德。孔子道："仁德的人付出一定的力量，然后收获果实，可以说是仁德了。"

23. 子曰："知者乐水，仁者乐山。知者动，仁者静。知者乐，仁者寿。"

孔子说："聪明人乐于水，仁人乐于山。聪明人活动，仁人沉静。聪明人快乐，仁人长寿。"

of it."

21. The Master said, "You can tell those who are above average about the best, but not those who are below average."

22. Fan Chi asked about wisdom. The Master said, "To work for the things the common people have a right to and to keep one's distance from the gods and spirits of the dead while showing them reverence can be called wisdom."

Fan Chi asked about benevolence. The Master said, "The benevolent man reaps the benefit only after encountering difficulties. That can be called benevolence."[6]

6. Cf. XII.22 where Confucius gives different answers to the same questions from Fan Chi.

23. The Master said, "The wise find joy in water; the benevolent find joy in mountains. The wise are active; the benevolent are still. The wise are joyful; the benevolent are long-lived."

24. 子曰："齐一变，至于鲁；鲁一变，至于道。"

孔子说："齐国［的政治和教育］一有改革，便达到鲁国的样子；鲁国［的政治和教育］一有改革，便进而合于大道了。"

25. 子曰："觚不觚，觚哉！觚哉！"

孔子说："觚不像个觚，*这是觚吗！这是觚吗！*"

26. 宰我问曰："仁者，虽告之曰：'井有仁焉。'其从之也？"

子曰："何为其然也？君子可逝也，不可陷也；可欺也，不可罔也。"

宰我问道："有仁德的人，就是告诉他：'井里掉下一位仁人啦。'他是不是会跟着下去呢？"

孔子道："为什么你要这样做呢？君子可以叫他远远走开不再回来，却不可以陷害他；可以欺骗他，却不可以愚弄他。"

27. 子曰："君子博学于文，约之以礼，亦可以弗畔矣夫！"

孔子说："君子广泛地学习文献，再用礼节来加以约束，

BOOK 6

24. The Master said, "At one stroke Qi can be made into a Lu, and Lu, at one stroke, can be made to attain the Way."

25. The Master said, "A *gu*[7] that is not truly a *gu*. *A gu indeed! A gu indeed!*"

7. a drinking vessel with a regulation capacity.

26. Zai Wo asked, "Even when he is told, 'There is a man in the well,' would a benevolent man go in search of him?"

The Master said, "Why should that be the case? A gentleman can be sent there, but cannot be lured into a trap. He can be deceived, but cannot be duped."

27. The Master said, "The gentleman widely versed in culture but brought back to essentials by the rites can, I suppose, be relied upon not to turn against what he stood for."

也就可以不至于离经叛道了。”

28. 子见南子，子路不说。夫子矢之曰：“予所否者，天厌之！天厌之！”

孔子去和南子相见，子路不高兴。孔子发誓道：“我假若不对的话，天厌弃我罢！天厌弃我罢！”

29. 子曰：“中庸之为德也，其至矣乎！民鲜久矣。”

孔子说：“中庸这种道德，该是最高的了，大家已经是长久地缺乏它了。”

30. 子贡曰：“如有博施于民而能济众，何如？可谓仁乎？”

子曰：“何事于仁！必也圣乎！尧舜其犹病诸！夫仁者，己欲立而立人，己欲达而达人。能近取譬，可谓仁之方也已。”

子贡道：“假若有这么一个人，广泛地给人民以好处，又能帮助大家生活得很好，怎么样？可以说是仁道了吗？”

孔子道：“哪里仅是仁道！那一定是圣德了！尧舜或者都难以做到哩！仁是什么呢？自己要站得住，同时也使别人站得住；自己要事事行得通，同时也使别人事事行得通。能

28. The Master went to see Nan Zi.[8] Zi–lu was displeased. The Master swore, "If I have done anything improper, may Heav–en's curse be on me, may Heaven's curse be on me! "

8. the notorious wife of Duke Ling of Wei.

29. The Master said, "Supreme indeed is the Mean as a moral virtue. It has long been rare among the common people."

30. Zi–gong said, "If there were a man who gave extensively to the common people and brought help to the multitude, what would you think of him? Could he be called benevolent?"

The Master said, "It is no longer a matter of benevolence with such a man. If you must describe him, 'sage' is, perhaps, the right word. Even Yao and Shun would have found it diffi–cult to accomplish as much. Now, on the other hand, a benev–olent man helps others to take their stand in that he himself wishes to take his stand, [9] and gets others there in that he himself wishes to get there. The ability to take as analogy what

够就眼下的事实选择例子一步步去做，可以说是实践仁道的方法了。”

is near at hand[10] can be called the method of benevolence."

9. It is with the help of the rites that one takes one's stand. Cf. "Take your stand through the help of the rites" (VIII.8) and "unless you study the rites you will be ill-equipped to take your stand" (XVI. 13).

10. viz., oneself.

述而篇第七

1. 子曰："述而不作，信而好古，窃比于我老彭。"

孔子说："阐述而不创作，以相信的态度喜爱古代文化，我私自和我那老彭相比。"

2. 子曰："默而识之，学而不厌，诲人不倦，何有于我哉？"

孔子说："[把所见所闻的]默默地记在心里，努力学习而不厌弃，教导别人而不疲倦，这些事情我做到了哪些呢？"

3. 子曰："德之不修，学之不讲，闻义不能徙，不善不能改，是吾忧也。"

孔子说："品德不培养；学问不讲习；听到义在那里，却不能亲身赴之；有缺点不能改正，这些都是我的忧虑哩！"

4. 子之燕居，申申如也，夭夭如也。

孔子在家闲居，很整齐的，很和乐而舒展的。

5. 子曰："甚矣吾衰也！久矣吾不复梦见周公！"

孔子说："我衰老得多么厉害呀！我好长时间没再梦见周

BOOK 7

1. The Master said, "I transmit but do not innovate; I am truthful in what I say and devoted to antiquity. I venture to compare myself to our Old Peng."[1]

1. It is not clear who Old Peng was.

2. The Master said, "Quietly to store up knowledge in my mind, to learn without flagging, to teach without growing weary. For me there is nothing to these things."

3. The Master said, "It is these things that cause me concern: failure to cultivate virtue, failure to go more deeply into what I have learned, inability, when I am told what is right, to go over to where it is, and inability to reform myself when I have defects."

4. During his leisure moments, the Master remained correct though relaxed.

5. The Master said, "How I have gone downhill! It has been such a long time since I dreamt of the Duke of Zhou."

公了！”

6. 子曰：“志于道，据于德，依于仁，游于艺。”

孔子说：“目标在‘道’，根据在‘德’，依靠在‘仁’，而游憩于礼、乐、射、御、书、数六艺之中。”

7. 子曰：“自行束脩以上，吾未尝无诲焉。”

孔子说：“只要是主动地给我一点见面薄礼，我从没有不教诲的。”

8. 子曰：“不愤不启，不悱不发。举一隅不以三隅反，则不复也。”

孔子说：“教导学生，不到他想求明白而不得的时候，不去开导他；不到他想说出来却说不出的时候，不去启发他。教给他东方，他却不能由此推知西、南、北三方，便不再教他了。”

9. 子食于有丧者之侧，未尝饱也。

孔子在死了亲属的人旁边吃饭，不曾吃饱过。

BOOK 7

6. The Master said, "I set my heart on the Way, base myself on virtue, lean upon benevolence for support and *take my recreation in the arts.*"

7. The Master said, "I have never denied instruction to anyone who, of his own accord, has given me so much as a bundle of dried meat as a present."

8. The Master said, "I never enlighten anyone who has not been driven to distraction by trying to understand a difficulty or who has not got into a frenzy trying to put his ideas into words.

"When I have pointed out one comer of a square to anyone and he does not come back with the other three, I will not point it out to him a second time."

9. When eating in the presence of one who had been bereaved, the Master never ate his fill.

10. 子于是日哭，则不歌。

孔子在这一天哭泣过，就不再唱歌。

11. 子谓颜渊曰：“用之则行，舍之则藏，惟我与尔有是夫！”

子路曰：“子行三军，则谁与？”

子曰：“暴虎冯河，死而无悔者，吾不与也。必也临事而惧，好谋而成者也。”

孔子对颜渊道：“用我呢，就干起来；不用呢，就藏起来。只有我和你才能这样吧！”

子路道：“您若率领军队，找谁共事？”

孔子道：“赤手空拳和老虎搏斗，不用船只去渡河，这样死了都不后悔的人，我是不和他共事的。[我所找他共事的，]一定是面临任务便恐惧谨慎，善于谋略而能完成的人哩！”

12. 子曰：“富而可求也，虽执鞭之士，吾亦为之。如不可求，从吾所好。”

孔子说：“财富如果可以求得的话，就是做市场的守门卒我也干。如果求它不到，还是我干我的罢。”

BOOK 7

10. On a day he had wept, the Master did not sing.

11. The Master said to Yan Yuan, "Only you and I have the ability to go forward when employed and to stay out of sight when set aside."[2]

Zi-lu said, "If you were leading the Three Armies whom would you take with you?"

The Master said, "I would not take with me anyone who would try to fight a tiger with his bare hands or to walk across *the River*[3] and die in the process without regrets. If I took anyone it would have to be a man who, when faced with a task, was fearful of failure and who, while fond of making plans, was capable of successful execution."

2. Cf. XV.7.

3. In ancient Chinese literature, "the River" meant the Yellow River.

12. The Master said, "If wealth were a permissible pursuit, I would be willing even to act as a guard holding a whip outside the market place. If it is not, I shall follow my own inclinations."

述而篇第七

13. 子之所慎：齐，战，疾。

孔子所小心慎重的事有三样：斋戒，战争，疾病。

14. 子在齐闻《韶》，三月不知肉味，曰："不图为乐之至于斯也。"

孔子在齐国听到《韶》的乐章，很长时间尝不出肉味，于是道："想不到欣赏音乐竟到了这种境界。"

15. 冉有曰："夫子为卫君乎？"子贡曰："诺；吾将问之。"

入，曰："伯夷、叔齐何人也？"

曰："古之贤人也。"

曰："怨乎？"

曰："求仁而得仁，又何怨？"

出，曰："夫子不为也。"

冉有道："老师赞成卫君吗？"子贡道："好罢；我去问问他。"

子贡进到孔子屋里，道："伯夷、叔齐是什么样的人？"

孔子道："是古代的贤人。"

子贡道："[他们两人互相推让，都不肯做孤竹国的国君，结果都跑到国外，]是不是后来又怨悔呢？"

孔子道："他们求仁德，便得到了仁德，又怨悔什么呢？"

13. Fasting, war and sickness were things with which the Master was careful.

14. The Master heard the *shao*[4] in Qi and for three months did not notice the taste of the meat he ate. He said, "I never dreamt that the joys of music could reach such heights."

4. the music of Shun. Cf. III.25.

15. Ran You said, "Is the Master on the side of the Lord of Wei?"[5] Zi-gong said, "Well, I shall put the question to him."

He went in and said, "What sort of men were Bo Yi and Shu Qi?"

"They were excellent men of old."

"Did they have any complaints?"

"They sought benevolence and got it. So why should they have any complaints?"

When Zi-gong came out, he said, "The Master is not on his side."

5. i.e., Zhe, known in history as the Ousted Duke, son of Prince Kuai Kui who was son of Duke Ling. After failing in an attempt to kill Nan Zi, the notorious wife of his father, Prince Kuai Kui fled to Qin. On the death of Duke

子贡走出，答复冉有道："老师不赞成卫君。"

16. 子曰："饭疏食饮水，曲肱而枕之，乐亦在其中矣。不义而富且贵，于我如浮云。"

孔子说："吃粗粮，喝冷水，弯着胳膊做枕头，也有着乐趣。干不正当的事而得来的富贵，我看来好像浮云。"

17. 子曰："加我数年，五十以学《易》，可以无大过矣。"

孔子说："让我多活几年，到五十岁的时候去学习《易》，便可以没有大过错了。"

18. 子所雅言，《诗》、《书》、执礼，皆雅言也。

孔子有用普通话的时候，读《诗》，读《书》，行礼，都用普通话。

19. 叶公问孔子于子路，子路不对。子曰："女奚不曰，其为人也，发愤忘食，乐以忘忧，不知老之将至云尔。"

叶公向子路问孔子为人怎么样，子路不回答。孔子对子路

Ling, Zhe came to the throne. With the backing of the Qin army, Prince Kuai Kui managed to install himself in the city of Qi in Wei, waiting for an opportunity to oust his son. At that time Confucius was in Wei, and what Ran You wanted to know was whether he was for Zhe.

16. The Master said, "In the eating of coarse rice and the drinking of water, the using of one's elbow for a pillow, joy is to be found. Wealth and rank attained through immoral means have as much to do with me as passing clouds."

17. The Master said, "Grant me a few more years so that I may continue *to learn* at the age of fifty and I shall, perhaps, be free from major errors."

18. What the Master used the correct pronunciation for was the *Odes*, the *Book of History* and the performance of the rites. In all these cases he used the correct pronunciation.

19. The Governor of She asked Zi-lu about Confucius. Zi-lu did not answer. The Master said, "Why did you not say something to this effect: he is the sort of man who forgets to eat when he

道:“你为什么不这样说:他的为人，用功便忘记吃饭，快乐便忘记忧愁，不晓得衰老会要到来，如此罢了。”

20. 子曰：“我非生而知之者，好古，敏以求之者也。”

孔子说:“我不是生来就有知识的人，而是爱好古代文化，勤奋敏捷去求得来的人。”

21. 子不语怪，力，乱，神。

孔子不谈怪异、勇力、叛乱和鬼神。

22. 子曰：“三人行，必有我师焉:择其善者而从之，其不善者而改之。”

孔子说:“几个人一块走路，其中便一定有可以为我所取法的人:我选取那些优点而学习，看出那些缺点而改正。”

23. 子曰：“天生德于予，桓魋其如予何?”

孔子说:“天在我身上生了这样的品德，那桓魋将把我怎样?”

works himself into a frenzy over some problem, who is so full of joy that he forgets his worries and who does not notice the onset of old age?"

20. The Master said, "I was not born with knowledge but, being fond of antiquity, I am quick to seek it."

21. The topics the Master did not speak of were prodigies, force, disorder and gods.

22. The Master said, "Even when walking in the company of two other men, I am bound to be able to learn from them. The good points of the one I copy; the bad points of the other I correct in myself."[6]

6. Cf. IV.17.

23. The Master said, "Heaven is author of the virtue that is in me. What can Huan Tui do to me?"[7]

7. According to tradition, this was said on the occasion when Huan Tui, the Minister of War in Song, attempted to kill him.

24. 子曰："二三子以我为隐乎?吾无隐乎尔。吾无行而不与二三子者，是丘也。"

孔子说："你们这些学生以为我有所隐瞒吗？我对你们是没有隐瞒的。我没有一点不向你们公开，这就是我孔丘的为人。"

25. 子以四教:文，行，忠，信。

孔子用四种内容教育学生:历代文献，社会生活的实践，对待别人的忠心，与人交际的信实。

26. 子曰："圣人，吾不得而见之矣；得见君子者，斯可矣。"

子曰："善人，吾不得而见之矣；得见有恒者，斯可矣。亡而为有，虚而为盈，约而为泰，难乎有恒矣。"

孔子说："圣人，我不能看见了；能看见君子，就可以了。"

又说："善人，我不能看见了；能看见有一定操守的人，就可以了。本来没有，却装做有；本来空虚，却装做充足；本来穷困，却要豪华，这样的人便难于保持一定操守了。"

27. 子钓而不纲，弋不射宿。

24. The Master said, "My friends, do you think I am secretive? There is nothing which I hide from you. There is nothing I do which I do not share with you, my friends. There is Qiu for you."

25. The Master instructs under four heads: culture, moral conduct, doing one's best and being trustworthy in what one says.

26. The Master said, "I have no hopes of meeting a sage. I would be content if I met someone who is a gentleman."

The Master said, "I have no hopes of meeting a good man. I would be content if I met someone who has constancy.[8] It is hard for a man to have constancy who claims to have when he is wanting, to be full when he is empty and to be comfortable when he is in straitened circumstances."

8. Cf. XIII.22.

27. The Master used a fishing line but not a cable;[9] he used a corded arrow but not to shoot at roosting birds.

孔子钓鱼，不用大绳横断流水来取鱼，用带生丝的箭射鸟，不射归巢的鸟。

28. 子曰：“盖有不知而作之者，我无是也。多闻，择其善者而从之；多见而识之；知之次也。”

孔子说：“大概有一种自己不懂却凭空造作的人，我没有这种毛病。多多地听，选择其中好的加以接受；多多地看，全记在心里。这样的知，是仅次于‘生而知之’的。”

29. 互乡难与言，童子见，门人惑。子曰：“与其进也，不与其退也，唯何甚?人洁已以进，与其洁也，不保其往也。”

互乡这地方的人难于交谈，一个童子得到孔子的接见，弟子们疑惑。孔子道：“我们赞成他的进步，不赞成他的退步，何必做得太过？别人把自己弄得干干净净而来，便应当赞成他的干净，不要死记住他那过去。”

9. to which a number of lines are attached.

28. The Master said, "There are presumably men who innovate without possessing knowledge, but that is not a fault I have. I use my ears widely and follow what is good in what I have heard; I use my eyes widely and retain what I have seen in my mind.[10] This constitutes a lower level of knowledge."[11]

10. Cf. XV.3.

11. Cf. "Those who are born with knowledge are the highest. Next come those who attain knowledge through study." (XVI.9)

29. People of Hu Xiang were difficult to talk to. A boy was received and the disciples were perplexed. The Master said, "Approval of his coming does not mean approval of him when he has withdrawn. Why should we be so exacting? When a man comes after having purified himself, we approve of his purification but we cannot vouch for his past."[12]

12. It has been suggested that this sentence should stand at the beginning of Confucius' remark.

30. 子曰："仁远乎哉？我欲仁，斯仁至矣。"

孔子道："仁德难道离我们很远吗？我要它，它就来了。"

31. 陈司败问昭公知礼乎，孔子曰："知礼。"

孔子退，揖巫马期而进之，曰："吾闻君子不党，君子亦党乎？君取于吴，为同姓，谓之吴孟子。君而知礼，孰不知礼？"

巫马期以告。子曰："丘也幸，苟有过，人必知之。"

陈司败向孔子问鲁昭公懂不懂礼，孔子道："懂礼。"

孔子走了出来，陈司败便向巫马期作了个揖，请他走近自己，然后说道："我听说君子无所偏袒，难道孔子竟偏袒吗？鲁君从吴国娶了位夫人，吴和鲁是同姓国家，［不便叫她做吴姬，］于是叫她做吴孟子。鲁君若是懂得礼，谁不懂得礼呢？"

巫马期把这话转告给孔子。孔子道："我真幸运，假若有错误，人家一定给指出来。"

BOOK 7

30. The Master said, "Is benevolence really far away? No sooner do I desire it than it is here."

31. Chen Si-bai asked whether Duke Zhao was versed in the rites. Confucius said, "Yes."

After Confucius had gone, Chen Si-bai, bowing to Wu-ma Qi, invited him forward and said, "I have heard that the gentleman does not show partiality. Does he show it nevertheless? The Lord took as wife a daughter of Wu, who thus is of the same clan as himself, [13] but he allows her to be called Wu Meng Zi.[14] If the Lord is versed in the rites, who isn't?"

When Wu-ma Qi recounted this to him, the Master said, "I am a fortunate man. Whenever I make a mistake, other people are sure to notice it."[15]

13. bearing the name Ji.

14. when she should be called Wu Ji 吴姬. Calling her Wu Meng Zi was an attempt to gloss over the fact that she shared the same clan name of Ji.

15. Being a native of Lu, Confucius would rather be criticized for partiality than appear to be openly critical of the Duke.

述而篇第七

32. 子与人歌而善，必使反之，而后和之。

孔子同别人一道唱歌，如果唱得好，一定请他再唱一遍，然后自己又和他。

33. 子曰："文，莫吾犹人也。躬行君子，则吾未之有得。"

孔子说："书本上的学问，大约我同别人差不多。在生活实践中做一个君子，那我还没有成功。"

34. 子曰："若圣与仁，则吾岂敢？抑为之不厌，诲人不倦，则可谓云尔已矣。"公西华曰："正唯弟子不能学也。"

孔子说道："讲到圣和仁，我怎么敢当？不过是学习和工作总不厌倦，教导别人总不疲劳，就是如此如此罢了。"公西华道："这正是我们学不到的。"

35. 子疾病，子路请祷。子曰："有诸？"

子路对曰："有之；《诔》曰：'祷尔于上下神祇。'"

子曰："丘之祷久矣。"

孔子病重，子路请求祈祷。孔子道："有这回事吗？"

子路答道："有的；《诔文》说过：'替你向天神地祇祈

32. While singing in the company of others, when the Master found a song attractive, he always asked to hear it again before joining in.

33. The Master said, "In unstinted effort I can compare with others, but in how to be a practising gentleman I can, as yet, claim no insight."

34. The Master said, "How dare I claim to be a sage or a benevolent man? Perhaps it might be said of me that I can keep at it without getting tired and go on teaching without growing weary."[16] Gong-xi Hua said, "This is precisely where we disciples are unable to learn from your example."

16. Cf. VIII.8. Mencius, II.A.2 (p. 59) contains what seems to be a fuller version of this passage.

35. The Master's illness became grave. Zi-lu asked permission to offer a prayer. The Master said, "Is there such a thing?"

Zi-lu said, "Yes, there is. The prayer offered is as follows: pray ye thus to the gods above and below."

The Master said, "In that case, I have long been offering my

祷。’”

孔子道：“我早就祈祷过了。”

36. 子曰：“奢则不孙，俭则固。与其不孙也，宁固。”

孔子说：“奢侈豪华就显得骄傲，省俭朴素就显得寒伧。与其骄傲，宁可寒伧。”

37. 子曰：“君子坦荡荡，小人长戚戚。”

孔子说：“君子心地平坦宽广，小人却经常局促忧愁。”

38. 子温而厉，威而不猛，恭而安。

孔子温和而严厉，有威仪而不凶猛，庄严而安详。

prayers."

36. The Master said, "Extravagance means ostentation, frugality means shabbiness. I would rather be shabby than ostentatious."

37. The Master said, "The gentleman is easy of mind, while the small man is ever full of anxiety."

38. The Master is cordial yet stem, awe–inspiring yet not fierce, and respectful yet at ease.

泰伯篇第八

1. 子曰："泰伯，其可谓至德也已矣。三以天下让，民无得而称焉。"

孔子说："泰伯，那可以说是品德极崇高了。屡次地把天下让给季历，老百姓简直找不出恰当的词语来称赞他。"

2. 子曰："恭而无礼则劳，慎而无礼则葸，勇而无礼则乱，直而无礼则绞。君子笃于亲，则民兴于仁；故旧不遗，则民不偷。"

孔子说："注重容貌态度的端庄，却不知礼，就未免劳倦；只知谨慎，却不知礼，就流于畏葸懦弱；专凭敢作敢为的胆量，却不知礼，就会盲动闯祸；心直口快，却不知礼，就会尖刻刺人。在上位的人能用深厚感情对待亲族，那老百姓就会走向仁德；在上位的人不遗弃他的老同事、老朋友，那老百姓就不致对人冷淡无情。"

3. 曾子有疾，召门弟子曰："启予足！启予手！《诗》云：'战战兢兢，如临深渊，如履薄冰。'而今而后，吾知免夫！小子！"

曾参病了，把他的学生召集拢来，说道："看看我的脚！看看我的手！《诗经》上说：'小心呀！谨慎呀！好像面临深

BOOK 8

1. The Master said, "Surely Tai Bo can be said to be of the highest virtue. Three times he abdicated his right to rule over the Empire, and yet he left behind nothing the common people could acclaim."[1]

1. Cf. "He was so boundless that the common people were not able to put a name to his virtues." (VIII. 19)

2. The Master said, "Unless a man has the spirit of the rites, in being respectful he will wear himself out, in being careful he will become timid, in having courage he will become unruly, and in being forthright he will become unrelenting.[2]

"When the gentleman feels profound affection for his parents, the common people will be stirred to benevolence. When he does not forget friends of long standing, the common people will not shirk their obligations to other people."

2. Cf. XVII.8.

3. When he was seriously ill Zeng Zi summoned his disciples and said, "Take a look at my hands. Take a look at my feet. The *Odes* say,

In fear and trembling,

深水坑之旁，好像行走薄薄冰层之上。’从今以后，我才晓得自己是可以免于祸害刑戮的了！学生们！”

4. 曾子有疾，孟敬子问之。曾子言曰：“鸟之将死，其鸣也哀；人之将死，其言也善。君子所贵乎道者三：动容貌，斯远暴慢矣；正颜色，斯近信矣；出辞气，斯远鄙倍矣。笾豆之事，则有司存。”

曾参病了，孟敬子探问他。曾子说：“鸟要死了，鸣声是悲哀的；人要死了，说出的话是善意的。在上位的人待人接物有三方面应该注重：严肃自己的容貌，就可以避免别人的粗暴和懈怠；端正自己的脸色，就容易使人相信；说话的时候，多考虑言辞和声调，就可以避免鄙陋粗野和错误。至于礼仪的细节，自有主管人员。”

5. 曾子曰：“以能问于不能，以多问于寡；有若无，实若虚；犯而不校——昔者吾友尝从事于斯矣。”

曾子说：“有能力却向无能力的人请教，知识丰富却向知

As if approaching a deep abyss,

As if walking on thin ice.[3]

Only now am I sure of being spared,[4] my young friends."

3. Ode 195.

4. i.e., to have avoided, now that he was on the point of death, the risk of the mutilation of his body—a duty which he owed to his parents.

4. Zeng Zi was seriously ill. When Meng Jing Zi visited him, this was what Zeng Zi said,

"Sad is the cry of a dying bird;

Good are the words of a dying man.

There are three things which the gentleman values most in the Way: to stay clear of violence by putting on a serious countenance, to come close to being trusted by setting a proper expression on his face, and to avoid being boorish and unreasonable by speaking in proper tones. As for the business of sacrificial vessels, there are officials whose concern this is."

5. Zeng Zi said, "To be capable yet to ask the advice of those who are not. To have many talents yet to ask the advice of those who have few. To have yet to appear to be wanting. To be

识缺少的人请教；有学问像没学问一样，满腹知识像空无所有一样；纵被欺侮，也不计较——从前我的一位朋友便曾这样做了。”

6. 曾子曰：“可以托六尺之孤，可以寄百里之命，临大节而不可夺也——君子人与?君子人也。”

曾子说：“可以把幼小的孤儿和国家的命脉都交付给他，面临安危存亡的紧要关头，却不动摇屈服——这种人，是君子人吗？是君子人哩。”

7. 曾子曰：“士不可以不弘毅，任重而道远。仁以为己任，不亦重乎？死而后已，不亦远乎？”

曾子说：“读书人不可以不刚强而有毅力，因为他负担沉重，路程遥远。以实现仁德于天下为己任，不也沉重吗？到死方休，不也遥远吗？”

8. 子曰：“兴于《诗》，立于礼，成于乐。”

孔子说：“诗篇使我振奋，礼使我能在社会上站得住，音

full yet to appear empty.[5] To be transgressed against yet not to mind. It was towards this end that my friend[6] used to direct his efforts."

5. This is in contrast to the man "who claims to have when he is wanting, to be full when he is empty" (VII.26).

6. According to tradition, this refers to Yan Hui.

6. Zeng Zi said, "If a man can be entrusted with an orphan six *chi*[7] tall, and the fate of a state one hundred *li* square, without his being deflected from his purpose even in moments of crisis, is he not a gentleman? He is, indeed, a gentleman."

7. The *chi* in Zeng Zi's time was much shorter than the modem foot.

7. Zeng Zi said, "A Gentleman must be strong and resolute, for his burden is heavy and the road is long. He takes benevolence as his burden. Is that not heavy? Only with death does the road come to an end. Is that not long?"

8. The Master said, "Be stimulated by the *Odes*, take your stand through the help of the rites[8] and be perfected by music."

乐使我的所学得以完成。"

9. 子曰："民可使由之，不可使知之。"

孔子说："老百姓，可以使他们照着我们的道路走去，不可以使他们知道那是为什么。"

10. 子曰："好勇疾贫，乱也。人而不仁，疾之已甚，乱也。"

孔子说："以勇敢自喜却厌恶贫困，是一种祸害。对于不仁的人，痛恨太甚，也是一种祸害。"

11. 子曰："如有周公之才之美，使骄且吝，其余不足观也已。"

孔子说："假如才能的美妙真比得上周公，只要骄傲而吝啬，别的方面也就不值得一看了。"

12. 子曰："三年学，不至于谷，不易得也。"

孔子说："读书三年并不存做官的念头，这是难得的。"

13. 子曰："笃信好学，守死善道。危邦不入，乱邦不居。天下有道则见，无道则隐。邦有道，贫且贱焉，耻也；邦无道，富

8. Cf. XX.3, XVI.3.

9. The Master said, "It is possible for the common people to be made to follow a policy, but it is not possible for them to be made to understand it."

10. The Master said, "Being fond of courage while detesting poverty will lead to insubordination. Excessive detestation of men who are not benevolent will provoke them to insubordination."

11. The Master said, "Even with a man as gifted as the Duke of Zhou, were he arrogant and miserly, then the rest of his qualities would not be worthy of admiration."

12. The Master said, "It is not easy to find a man who can study for three years without touching on the matter of salary."

13. The Master said, "Have firm faith and be fond of learning, and abide to the death in the good way. Enter not a state that is in

且贵焉，耻也。”

孔子说：“坚定地相信我们的道，努力学习它，誓死保全它。不进入危险的国家，不居住祸乱的国家。天下太平，就出来工作；不太平，就隐居。政治清明，自己贫贱，是耻辱；政治黑暗，自己富贵，也是耻辱。”

14. 子曰：“不在其位，不谋其政。”

孔子说：“不居于那个职位，便不考虑它的政务。”

15. 子曰：“师挚之始，《关雎》之乱，洋洋乎盈耳哉！”

孔子说：“当太师挚开始演奏的时候，当结尾演奏《关雎》之曲的时候，满耳朵都是音乐呀！”

16. 子曰：“狂而不直，侗而不愿，悾悾而不信，吾不知之矣。”

孔子说：“狂妄而不直率，幼稚而不老实，无能而不讲信用，这种人我是不知道其所以然的。”

peril; stay not in a state that is in danger. Let yourself be seen when the Way prevails in the Empire, but keep out of sight when it does not. It is a shameful matter to be poor and humble when the Way prevails in the state. Equally, it is a shameful matter to be rich and noble when the Way does not prevail in the state."

14. The Master said, "Do not concern yourself with matters of government unless they are the responsibility of the office you are in."[9]

9. This remark forms part of the saying in XIV.26.

15. The Master said, "When Zhi, the Master Musician, begins to play and when the *Guan ju*[10] comes to its end, how the sound fills the ear!"

10. the first ode in the *Odes*.

16. The Master said, "Men who reject discipline and yet are not straight, men who are ignorant and yet not cautious, men who are devoid of ability and yet not trustworthy are quite beyond my understanding."

泰伯篇第八

17. 子曰："学如不及，犹恐失之。"

孔子说："做学问好像［追逐什么似的，］生怕赶不上；［赶上了，］还生怕丢掉了。"

18. 子曰："巍巍乎，舜禹之有天下也而不与焉！"

孔子说："舜和禹真是崇高得很呀！贵为天子，富有四海，［却整年地为百姓勤劳，］一点也不为自己。"

19. 子曰："大哉尧之为君也！巍巍乎！唯天为大，唯尧则之。荡荡乎，民无能名焉。巍巍乎其有成功也，焕乎其有文章！"

孔子说："尧真是了不得呀！真高大得很呀！只有天最高最大，只有尧能够学习天。他的恩惠真是广博呀！老百姓简直不知道怎样称赞他。他的功绩实在太崇高了，他的礼仪制度也真够美好了！"

20. 舜有臣五人而天下治。武王曰："予有乱臣十人。"

孔子曰："才难，不其然乎？唐虞之际，于斯为盛。有妇人焉，九人而已。三分天下有其二，以服事殷。周之德，其可谓至德也已矣。"

舜有五位贤臣，天下便太平。武王也说过："我有十位能

17. The Master said, "Even when I spurred myself on in my studies as though I were lagging behind, *my fear was that I might not make it in time.*"

18. The Master said, "How lofty Shun and Yu were in holding aloof from the Empire when they were in possession of it."

19. The Master said, "Great indeed was Yao as a ruler! How lofty! It is Heaven that is great and it was Yao who modelled himself upon it. He was so boundless that the common people were not able to put a name to his virtues. Lofty was he in his successes and brilliant was he in his civilized accomplishments!"

20. Shun had five officials and the Empire was well governed. King Wu said, "I have ten capable officials."

Confucius commented, "How true it is that talent is difficult to come by! The period of Tang and Yu[11] was rich in talent.[12] With a woman amongst them, there were, in fact, only nine

治理天下的臣子。”

孔子因此说道:“[常言道:] ‘人才不易得。’不是这样吗?唐尧和虞舜之间以及周武王说那话的时候，人才最兴盛。然而武王十位人才之中还有一位妇女，实际上只是九位罢了。周文王得了天下的三分之二，仍然向商纣称臣，周朝的道德，可以说是最高的了。”

21. 子曰:“禹，吾无间然矣。菲饮食而致孝乎鬼神，恶衣服而致美乎黻冕，卑宫室而尽力乎沟洫。禹，吾无间然矣。”

孔子说:“禹，我对他没有批评了。他自己吃得很坏，却把祭品办得极丰盛；穿得很坏，却把祭服做得极华美；住得很坏，却把力量完全用于沟渠水利。禹，我对他没有批评了。”

men.[13] The Zhou continued to serve the Yin when it was in possession of twothirds of the Empire. Its virtue can be said to have been the highest."

11. Tang here is the name of Yao's dynasty and Yu the name of Shun's dynasty, not to be confused with Tang the founder of the Yin or Shang dynasty and Yu the founder of the Xia dynasty.
12. yet Shun had only five officials.
13. in the case of King Wu.

21. The Master said, "With Yu I can find no fault. He ate and drank the meanest fare while making offerings to ancestral spirits and gods with the utmost devotion proper to a descendant. He wore coarse clothes while sparing no effort to enhance the splendour of his robes and caps on sacrificial occasions. He lived in lowly dwellings while devoting all his energy to the building of irrigation canals. With Yu I can find no fault."

子罕篇第九

1. 子罕言利与命与仁。

孔子很少［主动］谈到功利、命运和仁德。

2. 达巷党人曰：“大哉孔子！博学而无所成名。”子闻之，谓门弟子曰：“吾何执？执御乎？执射乎？吾执御矣。”

达街的一个人说：“孔子真伟大！学问广博，可惜没有足以树立名声的专长。”孔子听了这话，就对学生们说：“我干什么呢？赶马车呢？做射击手呢？我赶马车好了。”

3. 子曰：“麻冕，礼也；今也纯，俭，吾从众。拜下，礼也；今拜乎上，泰也。虽违众，吾从下。”

孔子说：“礼帽用麻料来织，这是合于传统的礼的；今天大家都用丝料，这样省俭些，我同意大家的做法。臣见君，先在堂下磕头，然后升堂又磕头，这是合于传统的礼的。今天大家都免除了堂下的磕头，只升堂后磕头，这是倨傲的表现。虽然违反大家，我仍然主张要先在堂下磕头。”

4. 子绝四——毋意，毋必，毋固，毋我。

孔子一点也没有四种毛病——不悬空揣测，不绝对肯定，不拘泥固执，不唯我独是。

BOOK 9

1. The occasions on which the Master talked about profit, Destiny and benevolence were rare.

2. A man from a village in Da Xiang said, "Great indeed is Confucius! He has wide learning but has not made a name for himself in any field." The Master, on hearing of this, said to his disciples, "What should I make my speciality? Driving? or archery? I think I should prefer driving."

3. The Master said, "A ceremonial cap of linen is what is prescribed by the rites. Today black silk is used instead. This is more frugal and I follow the majority. To prostrate oneself before ascending the steps is what is prescribed by the rites. Today one does so after having ascended them. This is casual and, though going against the majority, I follow the practice of doing so before ascending."

4. There were four things the Master refused to have anything to do with: he refused to entertain conjectures[1] or insist on certainty;, he refused to be inflexible or to be egotistical.

1. Cf. "Is a man not superior who, without anticipating attempts at decep-

5. 子畏于匡，曰："文王既没，文不在兹乎？天之将丧斯文也，后死者不得与于斯文也；天之未丧斯文也，匡人其如予何？"

孔子被匡地的群众所拘禁，便道："周文王死了以后，一切文化遗产不都在我这里吗？天若是要消灭这种文化，那我也不会掌握这些文化了；天若是不要消灭这种文化，那匡人将把我怎么样呢？"

6. 太宰问于子贡曰："夫子圣者与？何其多能也？"子贡曰："固天纵之将圣，又多能也。"

子闻之，曰："太宰知我乎！吾少也贱，故多能鄙事。君子多乎哉？不多也。"

太宰向子贡问道："孔老先生是位圣人吗？为什么这样多才多艺呢？"子贡道："这本是上天让他成为圣人，又使他多才多艺。"

孔子听到，便道："太宰知道我呀！我小时候穷苦，所以学会了不少鄙贱的技艺。真正的君子会有这样多的技巧吗？是不会的。"

7. 牢曰："子云，'吾不试，故艺。'"

tion ... is, nevertheless, the first to be alerted to such behaviour?" (XIV.31)

5. When the Master met with danger in Kuang, he said, "With King Wen dead, is not culture (*wen*) invested here in me? If Heaven intends culture to be destroyed, those who come after me will not be able to have any part of it. If Heaven does not intend this culture to be destroyed, then what can the men of Kuang do to me?"

6. The *tai zai* [2] asked Zi-gong, "Surely the Master is a sage, is he not? Otherwise why is it he is skilled in so many things?" Zi-gong said, "It is true, Heaven set him on the path to sage-hood. However, he is, in addition, skilled in many things."

The Master, on hearing of this, said, "How well the *tai zai* knows me! I was of humble station when young. That is why I am skilled in many menial things. Should a gentleman be skilled in many things? No, not at all."

2. This is the title of a high office. It is not clear who the person referred to was or even from which state he came.

7. Lao[3] said, "The Master said, 'I have never been proved in of-

子罕篇第九

牢说："孔子说过，我不曾被国家所用，所以学得一些技艺。"

8. 子曰："吾有知乎哉?无知也。有鄙夫问于我，空空如也。我叩其两端而竭焉。"

孔子说："我有知识吗？没有哩。有一个庄稼汉问我，我本是一点也不知道的。我从他那个问题的首尾两头去盘问，[才得到很多意思,] 然后尽量地告诉他。"

9. 子曰："凤鸟不至，河不出图，吾已矣夫!"

孔子说："凤凰不飞来了，黄河也没有图画出来了，我这一生恐怕是完了吧！"

10. 子见齐衰者、冕衣裳者与瞽者，见之，虽少，必作；过之，必趋。

孔子看见穿丧服的人、穿戴着礼帽礼服的人以及瞎了眼睛的人，相见的时候，他们虽然年轻，孔子一定站起来；走过的时候，一定快走几步。

fice. That is why I am a jack of all trades.'"

3. The identity of the person referred to here is uncertain.

8. The Master said, "Do I possess knowledge? No, I do not. A rustic put a question to me and my mind was a complete blank. I kept hammering at the two sides of the question until I got everything out of it."[4]

4. The whole section is exceedingly obscure and the translation is tentative.

9. The Master said, "The Phoenix does not appear nor does the River offer up its Chart.[5] I am done for."

5. Both the Phoenix and the Chart were auspicious omens. Confucius is here lamenting the hopelessness of putting the Way into practice in the Empire of his day.

10. When the Master encountered men who were in mourning or had on ceremonial cap and robes or were blind, he would, on seeing them, rise to his feet, even though they were younger than he was, and, on passing them, would quicken his step.[6]

6. as a sign of respect.

子罕篇第九

11. 颜渊喟然叹曰："仰之弥高，钻之弥坚。瞻之在前，忽焉在后。夫子循循然善诱人，博我以文，约我以礼，欲罢不能。既竭吾才，如有所立卓尔。虽欲从之，末由也已。"

颜渊感叹着说："老师之道，越抬头看，越觉得高；越用力钻研，越觉得深。看看，似乎在前面，忽然又到后面去了。[虽然这样高深和不容易捉摸，可是]老师善于有步骤地诱导我们，用各种文献来丰富我的知识，又用一定的礼节来约束我的行为，使我想停止学习都不可能。我已经用尽我的才力，似乎能够独立地工作。要想再向前迈进一步，又不知怎样着手了。"

12. 子疾病，子路使门人为臣。病间，曰："久矣哉，由之行诈也！无臣而为有臣。吾谁欺?欺天乎!且予与其死于臣之手也，无宁死于二三子之手乎!且予纵不得大葬，予死于道路乎?"

孔子病得厉害，子路便命孔子的学生组织治丧处。很久以后，孔子的病渐渐好了，就道："仲由干这种欺假的勾当竟太长久了呀！我本不该有治丧的组织，却一定要使人组织治丧处。我欺哄谁呢？欺哄上天吗？我与其死在治丧的人的手里，宁肯死在你们学生的手里，不还好些吗？即使不能热热闹闹地办理丧葬，我会死在路上吗？"

11. Yan Yuan, heaving a sigh, said, "The more I look up at it the higher it appears. The more I bore into it the harder it becomes. I see it before me. Suddenly it is behind me.

"The Master is good at leading one on step by step. He broadens me with culture and brings me back to essentials by means of the rites. I cannot give up even if I wanted to, but, having done all I can, it[7] seems to rise sheer above me and I have no way of going after it, however much I may want to."

7. Throughout this chapter the "it" refers to the way of Confucius.

12. The Master's illness became grave. Zi-lu told his disciples to act as retainers.[8] During a period when his condition had improved, the Master said, "You has long been practising deception. In pretending that I had retainers when I had none, who would we be deceiving? Would we be deceiving Heaven? Moreover, would I not rather die in your hands, my friends, than in the hands of retainers? And even if I were not given an elaborate funeral, it is not as if I was dying by the wayside."

8. when Confucius, no longer in office, was not entitled to have them.

13. 子贡曰：“有美玉于斯，韫椟而藏诸？求善贾而沽诸？”子曰：“沽之哉！沽之哉！我待贾者也。”

子贡道：“这里有一块美玉，把它放在柜子里藏起来呢？还是找一个识货的商人卖掉呢？”孔子道：“卖掉！卖掉！我是在等待识货者哩。”

14 子欲居九夷。或曰：“陋，如之何？”子曰：“君子居之，何陋之有？”

孔子想搬到九夷去住。有人说：“那地方非常简陋，怎么好住？”孔子道：“有君子去住，就不简陋了。”

15. 子曰：“吾自卫反鲁，然后乐正，《雅》、《颂》各得其所。”

孔子说：“我从卫国回到鲁国，才把音乐［的篇章］整理出来，使《雅》归《雅》，《颂》归《颂》，各有适当的安置。”

16. 子曰：“出则事公卿，入则事父兄，丧事不敢不勉，不为酒困，何有于我哉？”

孔子说：“出外便服事公卿，入门便服事父兄，有丧事不

13. Zi–gong said, "If you had a piece of beautiful jade here, would you put it away safely in a box or would you try to sell it for a good price?"

The Master said, "Of course I would sell it. Of course I would sell it. All I am waiting for is the right offer."

14. The Master wanted to settle amongst the Nine Barbarian Tribes of the east. Someone said, "But could you put up with their uncouth ways?"

The Master said, "Once a gentleman settles amongst them, what uncouthness will there be?"

15. The Master said, "It was after my return from Wei to Lu that music was put right, with the *ya* and the *song*[9] being assigned their proper places."

9. The *ya* and the *song* are sections in the *Odes*.

16. The Master said, "To serve high officials when abroad, and my own elders when at home, in arranging funerals not to dare to spare myself, and to be able to hold my drink—For me, there is nothing to these at all."

敢不尽礼，不被酒所困扰，这些事我做到了哪些呢？”

17. 子在川上，曰：“逝者如斯夫！不舍昼夜。”

孔子在河边，叹道：“消逝的时光像河水一样呀！日夜不停地流去。”

18. 子曰：“吾未见好德如好色者也。”

孔子说：“我没有看见过这样的人，喜爱道德赛过喜爱美貌。”

19. 子曰：“譬如为山，未成一篑，止，吾止也。譬如平地，虽覆一篑，进，吾往也。”

孔子说：“好比堆土成山，只要再加一筐土便成山了，如果懒得做下去，这是我自己停止的。又好比在平地上堆土成山，纵是刚刚倒下一筐土，如果决心努力前进，还是要自己坚持啊！”

20. 子曰：“语之而不惰者，其回也与！”

孔子说：“听我说话始终不懈怠的，大概只有颜回一个人吧！”

17. While standing by a river, the Master said, "What passes away is, perhaps, like this. Day and night it never lets up."

18. The Master said, "I have yet to meet the man who is as fond of virtue as he is of beauty in women."[10]

10. This saying is repeated in XV.13.

19. The Master said, "As in the case of making a mound, if, before the very last basketful, I stop, then I shall have stopped. As in the case of levelling the ground, if, though tipping only one basketful, I am going forward, then I shall be making progress."

20. The Master said, "If anyone can listen to me with unflagging attention, it is Hui, I suppose."

21. 子谓颜渊，曰：“惜乎！吾见其进也，未见其止也。”

孔子谈到颜渊，说道：“可惜呀［他死了］！我只看见他不断地进步，*从没看见他停留*。”

22. 子曰：“苗而不秀者有矣夫！秀而不实者有矣夫！”

孔子说：“庄稼生长了，却不吐穗开花的，有过的罢！吐穗开花了，却不凝浆结实的，有过的罢！”

23. 子曰：“后生可畏，焉知来者之不如今也？四十、五十而无闻焉，斯亦不足畏也已。”

孔子说：“年少的人是可怕的，怎能断定他的将来赶不上现在的人呢？一个人到了四五十岁还没有什么名望，也就值不得惧怕了。”

24. 子曰：“法语之言，能无从乎？改之为贵。巽与之言，能无说乎？绎之为贵。说而不绎，从而不改，吾末如之何也已矣。”

孔子说：“严肃而合乎原则的话，能够不接受吗？改正错误才可贵。顺从己意的话，能够不高兴吗？分析一下才可贵。盲目高兴，不加分析；表面接受，实际不改，这种人我是没有办法对付他的了。”

21. The Master said of Yan Yuan, "I watched him make progress, *but I did not see him realize his capacity to the full.* What a pity!"

22. The Master said, "There are, are there not, young plants that fail to produce blossoms, and blossoms that fail to produce fruit?"

23. The Master said, "It is fitting that we should hold the young in awe. How do we know that the generations to come will not be the equal of the present? Only when a man reaches the age of forty or fifty without distinguishing himself in any way can one say, I suppose, that he does not deserve to be held in awe."

24. The Master said, "One cannot but give assent to exemplary words, but what is important is that one should rectify oneself. One cannot but be pleased with tactful words, but what is important is that one should reform oneself. I can do nothing with the man who gives assent but does not rectify himself or the man who is pleased but does not reform himself."

子罕篇第九

25. 子曰："主忠信，毋友不如己者，过则勿惮改。"

26. 子曰："三军可夺帅也，匹夫不可夺志也。"

孔子说："一国军队，可以使它丧失主帅；一个男子汉，却不能强迫他放弃主张。"

27. 子曰："衣敝缊袍，与衣狐貉者立，而不耻者，其由也与？'不忮不求，何用不臧？'"子路终身诵之。子曰："是道也，何足以臧？"

孔子说道："穿着破烂的旧丝绵袍子和穿着狐貉裘的人一道站着，不觉得惭愧的，恐怕只有仲由罢！《诗经》上说：'不嫉妒，不贪求，为什么不会好？'"子路听了，便老念着这两句诗。孔子又道："仅仅这个样子，怎样能够好得起来？"

28. 子曰："岁寒，然后知松柏之后凋也。"

25. The Master said, "Make it your guiding principle to do your best for others and to be trustworthy in what you say. Do not accept as friend anyone who is not as good as you. When you make a mistake, do not be afraid of mending your ways." [11]

11. This saying has already appeared as part of 1.8.

26. The Master said, "The Three Armies can be deprived of their commander, but there is no way a common man can be deprived of his purpose."

27. The Master said, "If anyone can, while dressed in a worn-out gown padded with old silk floss, stand beside a man wearing fox or badger fur without feeling ashamed, it is, I suppose, You.

Neither envious nor covetous,
How can he be anything but good?"[12]

Thereafter, Zi-lu constantly recited these verses. The Master commented, "The way summed up in these verses will hardly enable one to be good."

12. Ode 33.

28. The Master said, "Only when the cold season comes is the

子罕篇第九

孔子说："天冷了，才晓得松柏树是最后落叶的。"

29. 子曰："知者不惑，仁者不忧，勇者不惧。"

孔子说："聪明的人不致疑惑，仁德的人经常乐观，勇敢的人无所畏惧。"

30. 子曰："可与共学，未可与适道；可与适道，未可与立；可与立，未可与权。"

孔子说："可以同他一道学习的人，未必可以同他一道取得某种成就；可以同他一道取得某种成就的人，未必可以同他一道事事依礼而行；可以同他一道事事依礼而行的人，未必可以同他一道通权达变。"

31. "唐棣之华，偏其反而。岂不尔思？室是远而。"子曰："未之思也，夫何远之有？"

point brought home that the pine and the cypress are the last to lose their leaves."

29. The Master said, "The man of wisdom is never in two minds;[13] the man of benevolence never worries;[14] the man of courage is never afraid."[15]

13. about right and wrong.

14. about the future.

15. This chapter forms part of XIV.28 where the saying about the man of benevolence comes before the one about the man of wisdom.

30. The Master said, "A man good enough as a partner in one's attempt to learn need not be good enough as a partner in the pursuit of the Way; a man good enough as a partner in the pursuit of the Way need not be good enough as a partner in a common stand; a man good enough as a partner in a common stand need not be good enough as a partner in the exercise of moral discretion."

31. The flowers of the cherry tree,
How they wave about!

子罕篇第九

古代有几句这样的诗:“唐棣树的花,翩翩地摇摆。难道我不想念你?因为家住得太遥远。”孔子道:“他是不去想念哩,真的想念,有什么遥远呢?”

It's not that I do not think of you,
But your home is so far away.[16]

The Master commented, "He did not really think of her. If he did, there is no such thing as being far away."

16. These lines are not to be found in the present *Odes*.

乡党篇第十

1. 孔子于乡党，恂恂如也，似不能言者。其在宗庙朝廷，便便言，唯谨尔。

孔子在本乡的地方上非常恭顺，好像不能说话的样子。

他在宗庙里、朝廷上，有话便明白而流畅地说出，只是说得很少。

2. 朝，与下大夫言，侃侃如也；与上大夫言，訚訚如也。君在，踧踖如也，与与如也。

上朝的时候，［君主还没有到来，］同下大夫说话，温和而快乐的样子；同上大夫说话，正直而恭敬的样子。君主已经来了，恭敬而心中不安的样子，行步安详的样子。

3. 君召使摈，色勃如也，足躩如也。揖所与立，左右手，衣前后，襜如也。趋进，翼如也。宾退，必复命曰："宾不顾矣。"

鲁君召他去接待外国的贵宾，面色矜持庄重，脚步也快起来。向两旁的人作揖，或者向左拱手，或者向右拱手，衣裳一俯一仰，却很整齐。快步向前，好像鸟儿舒展了翅膀。贵宾辞别后一定向君主回报说："客人已经不回头了。"

4. 入公门，鞠躬如也，如不容。

BOOK 10

1. In the local community, Confucius was submissive and seemed to be inarticulate. In the ancestral temple and at court, though fluent, he did not speak lightly.

2. At court, when speaking with Counsellors of lower rank, he was affable; when speaking with Counsellors of upper rank, he was frank though respectful. In the presence of his lord, his bearing, though respectful, was composed.

3. When he was summoned by his lord to act as usher, his face took on a serious expression and his step became brisk. When he bowed to his colleagues, stretching out his hands to the left or to the right, his robes followed his movements without being disarranged. He went forward with quickened steps, as though he was gliding on wings. After the withdrawal of the guest, he invariably reported, "The guest has stopped looking back."

4. On going through the outer gates to his lord's court, he drew

乡党篇第十

立不中门，行不履阈。

过位，色勃如也，足躩如也，其言似不足者。

摄齐升堂，鞠躬如也，屏气似不息者。

出，降一等，逞颜色，怡怡如也。

没阶，趋进，翼如也。

复其位，踧踖如也。

孔子走进朝廷的门，害怕而谨慎的样子，好像没有容身之地。

站，不站在门的中间；走，不踩门坎。

经过国君的座位，面色便矜庄，脚步也快，言语也好像中气不足。

提起下摆向堂上走，恭敬谨慎的样子，憋住气好像不呼吸一般。

走出来，降下台阶一级，面色便放松，怡然自得。

走完了台阶，快快地向前走几步，好像鸟儿舒展翅膀。

回到自己的位置，恭敬而内心不安的样子。

5. 执圭，鞠躬如也，如不胜。上如揖，下如授。勃如战色，足蹜蹜如有循。

享礼，有容色。

私觌，愉愉如也。

［孔子出使到外国，举行典礼，］拿着圭，恭敬谨慎地，

himself in, as though the entrance was too small to admit him.

When he stood, he did not occupy the centre of the gateway;[1] when he walked, he did not step on the threshold.

When he went past the station of his lord, his face took on a serious expression, his step became brisk, and his words seemed more laconic.

When he lifted the hem of his robe to ascend the hall, he drew himself in, stopped inhaling as if he was no longer breathing.

When he had come out and descended the first step, relaxing his expression, he seemed no longer to be tense.

When he had reached the bottom of the steps he went forward with quickened steps as though he was gliding on wings.

When he resumed his station, his bearing was respectful.

1. A position which would have been presumptuous.

5. When he held the jade tablet, he drew himself in as though its weight was too much for him. He held the upper part of the tablet as though he was bowing; he held the lower part of the tablet as though he was ready to hand over a gift. His expression was solemn as though in fear and trembling, and his feet

好像举不起来。向上举好像在作揖，向下拿好像在交给别人。面色矜庄好像在作战。脚步也紧凑狭窄，好像在沿着［一条线］走过。

献礼物的时候，满脸和气。

用私人身份和外国君臣会见，显得轻松愉快。

6. 君子不以绀緅饰，红紫不以为亵服。

当暑，袗絺绤，必表而出之。

缁衣，羔裘；素衣，麑裘；黄衣，狐裘。

亵裘长，短右袂。

必有寝衣，长一身有半。

狐貉之厚以居。

去丧，无所不佩。

非帷裳，必杀之。

羔裘玄冠不以吊。

吉月，必朝服而朝。

君子不用［近乎黑色的］天青色和铁灰色作镶边，［近乎赤色的］浅红色和紫色不用来作平常居家的衣服。

暑天，穿着粗的或者细的葛布单衣，但一定裹着衬衫，使它露在外面。

黑色的衣配紫羔，白色的衣配麑裘，黄色的衣配狐裘。

were constrained as though following a marked line.

When making a presentation, his expression was genial.

At a private audience, he was relaxed.

6. The gentleman avoided using dark purple, and maroon coloured silk for lapels and cuffs. Red and violet coloured silks were not used for informal dress.

When, in the heat of summer, he wore an unlined robe made of either fine or coarse material, he invariably wore it over an underrobe to set it off.

Under a black jacket, he wore lambskin; under an undyed jacket, he wore fawnskin; under a yellow jacket, he wore fox fur.

His informal fur coat was long but with a short right sleeve.

He invariably had a night shirt which came down to his knees.[2]

Their fur being thick, pelts of the fox and the badger were used as rugs.

Once the period of mourning was over, he placed no restric-

乡党篇第十

居家的皮袄身材较长，可是右边的袖子要做得短些。

睡觉一定有小被，长度合本人身长的一又二分之一。

用狐貉皮的厚毛作坐垫。

丧服满了以后，什么东西都可以佩带。

不是[上朝和祭祀穿的]用整幅布做的裙子，一定裁去一些布。

紫羔和黑色礼帽都不穿戴着去吊丧。

大年初一，一定穿着上朝的礼服去朝贺。

7. 齐，必有明衣，布。

齐必变食，居必迁坐。

斋戒沐浴的时候，一定有浴衣，用布做的。

斋戒的时候，一定改变平常的饮食；居住也一定搬移地方[不和妻妾同房]。

8. 食不厌精，脍不厌细。

食饐而餲，鱼馁而肉败，不食。色恶，不食。臭恶，不食。失饪，不食。不时，不食。割不正，不食。不得其酱，不食。

肉虽多，不使胜食气。

唯酒无量，不及乱。

tions on the kind of ornament that he wore.

Other than skirts for ceremonial occasions, everything else was made up from cut pieces.

Lambskin coats and black caps were not used on visits of condolence.

On New Year's Day, he invariably went to court in court dress.

2. It has been suggested that this sentence has got out of place and should follow the first sentence in the next section.

7. In periods of purification, he invariably wore a house robe made of the cheaper sort of material.

In periods of purification, he invariably changed to a more austere diet and, when at home, did not sit in his usual place.

8. He did not eat his fill of polished rice, nor did he eat his fill of finely minced meat.

He did not eat rice that had gone sour or fish and meat that had spoiled. He did not eat food that had gone off colour or food that had a bad smell. He did not eat food that was not

沽酒市脯不食。

不撤姜食，不多食。

粮食不嫌舂得精，鱼和肉不嫌切得细。

粮食霉烂发臭，鱼和肉腐烂，都不吃。食物颜色难看，不吃。气味难闻，不吃。烹调不当，不吃。不到该当吃食的时候，不吃。不是按一定方法砍割的肉，不吃。没有一定调味的酱醋，不吃。

席上肉虽然多，吃它不超过主食。

只有酒不限量，却不至醉。

买来的酒和肉干不吃。

吃完了，姜不撤除，但吃得不多。

9. 祭于公，不宿肉。祭肉不出三日。出三日，不食之矣。

参与国家祭祀典礼，不把祭肉留到第二天。别的祭肉留存不超过三天。若是存放过了三天，便不吃了。

10. 食不语，寝不言。

吃饭的时候不交谈，睡觉的时候不说话。

11. 虽疏食菜羹，瓜祭，必齐如也。

properly prepared nor did he eat except at the proper times. He did not eat food that had not been properly cut up, nor did he eat unless the proper sauce was available.

Even when there was plenty of meat, he avoided eating more meat than rice.

Only in the case of wine did he not set himself a rigid limit. He simply never drank to the point of becoming confused.

He did not consume wine or dried meat bought from a shop.

Even when he did not have the side dish of ginger cleared from the table, he did not eat more than was proper.

9. After assisting at a sacrifice at his lord's place, he did not keep his portion of the sacrificial meat overnight. In other cases, he did not keep the sacrificial meat for more than three days. Once it was kept beyond three days he no longer ate it.

10. He did not converse at meals; nor did he talk in bed.

11. Even when a meal consisted only of coarse rice and vegetable

虽然是糙米饭小菜汤，也一定得先祭一祭，而且祭的时候还一定恭恭敬敬，好像斋戒了的一样。

12. 席不正，不坐。

坐席摆的方向不合礼制，不坐。

13. 乡人饮酒，杖者出，斯出矣。

行乡饮酒礼后，要等老年人都出去了，自己这才出去。

14. 乡人傩，朝服而立于阼阶。

本地方人迎神驱鬼，穿着朝服站在东边的台阶上。

15. 问人于他邦，再拜而送之。

托人给在外国的朋友问好送礼，便向受托者拜两次送行。

16. 康子馈药，拜而受之。曰："丘未达，不敢尝。"

季康子给孔子送药，孔子拜而接受，却说道："我对这药性不很了解，不敢试服。"

17. 厩焚。子退朝，曰："伤人乎？"不问马。

broth, he invariably made an offering from them and invariably did so solemnly.

12. He did not sit, unless his mat was straight.

13. When drinking at a village gathering, he left as soon as those carrying walking sticks had left.

14. When the villagers were exorcizing evil spirits, he stood in his court robes on the eastern steps.[3]

3. the place for a host to stand.

15. When making inquiries after someone in another state, he bowed to the ground twice before sending off the messenger.

16. When Kang Zi sent a gift of medicine, bowed his head to the ground before accepting it. However, he said, "Not knowing its properties, I dare not taste it."

17. The stables caught fire. The Master, on returning from court,

孔子的马棚失了火。孔子从朝廷回来，道："伤了人吗？"不问到马。

18. 君赐食，必正席先尝之。君赐腥，必熟而荐之。君赐生，必畜之。侍食于君，君祭，先饭。

国君赐以熟食，孔子一定摆正座位先尝一尝。国君赐以生肉，一定煮熟了，先［给祖宗］进供。国君赐以活物，一定养着它。

同国君一道吃饭，当他举行饭前祭礼的时候，自己先吃饭，［不吃菜。］

19. 疾，君视之，东首，加朝服，拖绅。

孔子病了，国君来探问，他便脑袋朝东，把上朝的礼服披在身上，拖着大带。

20. 君命召，不俟驾行矣。

国君呼唤，孔子不等待车辆驾好马，立即先步行。

21. 入太庙，每事问。

asked, "Was anyone hurt?" He did not ask about the horses.

18. When his lord gave a gift of cooked food, the first thing he invariably did was to taste it after having adjusted his mat. When his lord gave him a gift of uncooked food, he invariably cooked it and offered it to the ancestors. When his lord gave him a gift of a live animal, he invariably reared it. At the table of his lord, when his lord had made an offering before the meal he invariably started with the rice first.

19. During an illness, when his lord paid him a visit, he would lie with his head to the east, with his court robes draped over him and his grand sash trailing over the side of the bed.

20. When summoned by his lord, he would set off without waiting for horses to be yoked to his carriage.

21. When he went inside the Grand Temple, he asked questions about everything .[4]

4. This forms part of Ⅲ. 15.

22. 朋友死，无所归，曰："于我殡。"

朋友死亡，没有负责收殓的人，孔子便道："丧葬由我来料理。"

23. 朋友之馈，虽车马，非祭肉，不拜。

朋友的赠品，即使是车马，只要不是祭肉，孔子在接受的时候，不行礼。

24. 寝不尸，居不客。

孔子睡觉不像死尸一样［直躺着］，平日坐着，也不像接见客人或者自己做客人一样，［跪着两膝在席上。］

25. 见齐衰者，虽狎，必变。见冕者与瞽者，虽亵，必以貌。
凶服者式之。式负版者。
有盛馔，必变色而作。
迅雷风烈必变。

孔子看见穿齐衰孝服的人，就是极亲密的，也一定改变态度，［表示同情。］看见戴着礼帽和瞎了眼睛的人，即使常相见，也一定有礼貌。

BOOK 10

22. Whenever a friend died who had no kin to whom his body could be taken, he said, "Let him be given a funeral from my house."

23. Even when a gift from a friend was a carriage and horses—since it lacked the solemnity of sacrificial meat—he did not bow to the ground.

24. When in bed, he did not lie like a corpse, nor did he sit in the formal manner of a guest when by himself.

25. When he met a bereaved person in mourning dress, even though it was someone he was on familiar terms with, he invariably assumed a solemn expression. When he met someone wearing a ceremonial cap or someone blind, even though they were wellknown to him, he invariably showed them respect.[5]

On passing a person dressed as a mourner he would lean forward with his hands on the cross-bar of his carriage to show

在车中遇着拿了送死人衣物的人，便把身体微微地向前一俯，手伏着车前的横木，[表示同情。]遇见背负国家图籍的人，也手伏车前横木。

一有丰富的菜肴，一定神色变动，站立起来。

遇见疾雷、大风，一定改变态度。

26. 升车，必正立，执绥。

车中，不内顾，不疾言，不亲指。

孔子上车，一定先端正地站好，拉着扶手带[登车]。

在车中，不向内回顾，不很快地说话，不用手指指画画。

27. 色斯举矣，翔而后集。曰："山梁雌雉，时哉时哉！"子路共之，三嗅而作。

[孔子在山谷中行走，看见几只野鸡。]孔子的脸色一动，野鸡便飞向天空，盘旋一阵，又都停在一处。孔子道："这些山梁上的雌雉，得其时呀！得其时呀！"子路向它们拱拱手，它们又振一振翅膀飞去了。

respect; he would act in a similar manner towards a person carrying official documents.

When a sumptuous feast was brought on, he invariably assumed a solemn expression and rose to his feet.

When there was a sudden clap of thunder or a violent wind, he invariably assumed a solemn attitude.

5. Cf. IX.10.

26. When climbing into a carriage, he invariably stood squarely and grasped the mounting-cord.

When in the carriage, he did not turn towards the inside, nor did he shout or point.

27. Startled, the bird rose up and circled round before alighting. He said, "The female pheasant on the mountain bridge, how timely her action is, how timely her action is!" Zi-lu cupped one hand in the other in a gesture of respect towards the bird which, flapping its wings three times, flew away.

先进篇第十一

1. 子曰："先进于礼乐，野人也；后进于礼乐，君子也。如用之，则吾从先进。"

孔子说："先学习礼乐而后做官的是未曾有过爵禄的一般人，先有了官位而后学习礼乐的是卿大夫的子弟。如果要我选用人才，我主张选用先学习礼乐的人。"

2. 子曰："从我于陈、蔡者，皆不及门也。"

孔子说："跟着我在陈国、蔡国之间忍饥受饿的人，都不在我这里了。"

3. 德行:颜渊，闵子骞，冉伯牛，仲弓。言语:宰我，子贡。政事:冉有，季路。文学:子游，子夏。

[孔子的学生各有所长。]德行好的:颜渊，闵子骞，冉伯牛，仲弓。会说话的:宰我，子贡。能办理政事的:冉有，季路。熟悉古代文献的:子游，子夏。

4. 子曰："回也非助我者也，于吾言无所不说。"

孔子说："颜回不是对我有所帮助的人，他对我的话没有不喜欢的。"

BOOK 11

1. The Master said, "*As far as the rites and music are concerned, the disciples who were the first to come to me were rustics while those who came to me afterwards were gentlemen. When it comes to putting the rites and music to use, I follow the former.*"

2. The Master said, "None of those who were with me in Chen and Cai ever got as far as my door."[1]

1. This is a most puzzling saying however it is interpreted.

3. Virtuous conduct: Yan Yuan, Min Zi–qian, Ran Bo–niu and Zhong–gong; speech: Zai Wo and Zi–gong; government: Ran You and Ji–lu; culture and learning: Zi–you and Zi–xia.

4. The Master said, "Hui is no help to me at all. He is pleased with everything I say."

5. 子曰："孝哉闵子骞！人不间于其父母昆弟之言。"

孔子说："闵子骞真是孝顺呀！别人对于他爹娘兄弟称赞他的言语并无异议。"

6. 南容三复白圭，孔子以其兄之子妻之。

南容把"白圭之玷，尚可磨也；斯言之玷，不可为也"的几句诗读了又读，孔子便把自己的侄女嫁给他。

7. 季康子问："弟子孰为好学？"孔子对曰："有颜回者好学，不幸短命死矣，今也则亡。"

季康子问道："你学生中谁用功？"孔子答道："有一个叫颜回的用功，不幸短命死了，现在就再没有这样的人了。"

5. The Master said, "What a good son Min Zi-qian is! No one can find fault with what his parents and brothers have to say about him."

6. Nan Rong repeated over and over again the lines about the white jade sceptre.[2] Confucius gave him his elder brother's daughter in marriage.[3]

2. i.e., the lines from Ode 256 which run as follows:

   A blemish on the white jade
   Can still be polished away;
   A blemish on these words
   Cannot be removed at all.

3. Cf. V.2.

7. Ji Kang Zi asked which of his disciples was eager to learn.

Confucius answered, "There was one Yan Hui who was eager to learn, but unfortunately his allotted span was a short one and he died. Now there is no one."[4]

4. Cf. VI.3 where a similar conversation between Duke Ai of Lu and Confucius is to be found.

先进篇第十一

8. 颜渊死，颜路请子之车以为之椁。子曰："才不才，亦各言其子也。鲤也死，有棺而无椁。吾不徒行以为之椁。以吾从大夫之后，不可徒行也。"

颜渊死了，他父亲颜路请求孔子卖掉车子来替颜渊办外椁。孔子道："不管有才能或者没有才能，但总是自己的儿子。我的儿子鲤死了，也只有内棺，没有外椁。我不能［卖掉车子］步行来替他买椁。因为我也曾做过大夫，是不可以步行的。"

9. 颜渊死。子曰："噫！天丧予！天丧予！"

颜渊死了，孔子道："咳！天老爷要我的命呀！天老爷要我的命呀！"

10. 颜渊死，子哭之恸。从者曰："子恸矣！"曰："有恸乎？非夫人之为恸而谁为？"

颜渊死了，孔子哭得很伤心。跟着孔子的人道："您太伤心了！"孔子道："真的太伤心了吗？我不为这样的人伤心，还为什么人伤心呢！"

11. 颜渊死，门人欲厚葬之。子曰："不可。"

8. When Yan Yuan died, Yan Lu[5] asked the Master to give him his carriage to provide for an outer coffin for his son. The Master said, "Everyone speaks up for his own son whether he is talented or not. When Li[6] died, he had a coffin but no outer coffin, I did not go on foot in order to provide him with an outer coffin, because it would not have been proper for me to go on foot, seeing that I took my place after the Counsellors."

5. Yan Yuan's father.

6. Confucius' son.

9. When Yan Yuan died, the Master said, "Alas! Heaven has bereft me! Heaven has bereft me!"

10. When Yan Yuan died, in weeping for him, the Master showed undue sorrow. His followers said, "You are showing undue sorrow."

"Am I? Yet if not for him, for whom should I show undue sorrow?"

11. When Yan Yuan died, the disciples wanted to give him a lav-

先进篇第十一

门人厚葬之。子曰："回也视予犹父也，予不得视犹子也。非我也，夫二三子也。"

颜渊死了，孔子的学生们想要很丰厚地埋葬他。孔子道："不可以。"

学生们仍然很丰厚地埋葬了他。孔子道："颜回呀！你看待我好像看待父亲，我却不能够像对待儿子一般地看待你。这不是我的主意呀，是你那班同学干的呀。"

12. 季路问事鬼神。子曰："未能事人，焉能事鬼？"

曰："敢问死。"

曰："未知生，焉知死？"

子路问服事鬼神的方法。孔子道："活人还不能服事，怎么能去服事死人？"

子路又道："我大胆地请问死是怎么回事。"孔子道："生的道理还没有弄明白，怎么能够懂得死？"

13. 闵子侍侧，訚訚如也；子路，行行如也；冉有、子贡，侃侃如也。子乐。

"若由也，不得其死然。"

闵子骞站在孔子身旁，恭敬而正直的样子；子路很刚强的样子；冉有、子贡温和而快乐的样子。孔子高兴起来了。

ish burial. The Master said, "It would not be proper."

All the same, they gave him a lavish burial. The Master said, "Hui treated me as a father, yet I have been prevented from treating him as a son. This was none of my choice. It was the doing of these others."

12. Ji-lu asked how the spirits of the dead and the gods should be served. The Master said, "You are not able even to serve man. How can you serve the spirits?"

"May I ask about death?"

"You do not understand even life. How can you understand death?"

13. When in attendance on the Master, Min Zi looked respectful and upright; Zi-lu looked unbending; Ran You and Zi-gong looked affable. The Master was happy.

"A man like You will not die a natural death."[7]

7. This remark seems out of place here. It probably belongs to another

[不过，又道:] “像仲由吧，怕得不到好死。”

14. 鲁人为长府。闵子骞曰：“仍旧贯，如之何?何必改作?”

子曰：“夫人不言，言必有中。”

鲁国翻修叫长府的金库。闵子骞道:“照着老样子下去怎么样?为什么一定要翻造呢?”孔子道:“这个人平日不大开口，一开口一定中肯。”

15. 子曰：“由之瑟奚为于丘之门?”门人不敬子路。子曰：“由也升堂矣，未入于室也。”

孔子道:“仲由弹瑟，为什么在我这里来弹呢?”因此孔子的学生们瞧不起子路。孔子道:“由么，学问已经不错了，只是还不够精深罢了。”

16. 子贡问：“师与商也孰贤?”

子曰：“师也过，商也不及。”

曰：“然则师愈与?”

子曰：“过犹不及。”

子贡问孔子:“颛孙师(子张)和卜商（子夏）两个人，谁强一些?”孔子道:“师呢，有些过分；商呢，有些赶不上。”

子贡道:“那么，师强一些吗?”孔子道:“过分和赶不上同

context.

14. The people of Lu were rebuilding the treasury. Min Zi-qian said, "Why not simply restore it? Why must it be totally rebuilt?"

The Master said, "Either this man does not speak or he says something to the point."

15. The Master said, "What is You's lute doing inside my door?" The disciples ceased to treat Zi-lu with respect. The Master said, "You may not have entered the inner room, but he has ascended the hall."

16. Zi-gong asked, "Who is superior, Shi or Shang?"

The Master said, "Shi overshoots the mark; Shang falls short."

"Does that mean that Shi is in fact better?"

The Master said, "There is little to choose between overshooting the mark and falling short."

样不好。”

17. 季氏富于周公，而求也为之聚敛而附益之。子曰：“非吾徒也。小子鸣鼓而攻之，可也。”

季氏比周公还有钱，冉求却又替他搜括，增加更多的财富。孔子道：“冉求不是我们的人，你们学生很可以大张旗鼓地来攻击他。”

18. 柴也愚，参也鲁，师也辟，由也喭。

高柴愚笨，曾参迟钝，颛孙师偏激，仲由卤莽。

19. 子曰：“回也其庶乎，屡空。赐不受命，而货殖焉，亿则屡中。”

孔子说：“颜回的学问道德差不多了罢，可是常常穷得没有办法。端木赐不安本分，去囤积投机，猜测行情，竟每每猜对了。”

20. 子张问善人之道。子曰：“不践迹，亦不入于室。”

子张问怎样才是善人。孔子道：“善人不踩着别人的脚印

17. The wealth of the Ji family was greater than that of the Duke of Zhou, and still Qiu helped them add further to that wealth by raking in the taxes. The Master said, "He is no disciple of mine. You, my young friends, may attack him openly to the beating of drums."[8]

8. Cf. Mencius, IV.A.14.

18. "Chai is stupid; Can is slow; Shi is onesided; You is forthright."

19. The Master said, "Hui is perhaps difficult to improve upon; he allows himself constantly to be in dire poverty. Ci refuses to accept his lot and indulges in moneymaking, and is frequently right in his conjectures."

20. Zi-zhang asked about the way of the good man. The Master said, "Such a man does not follow in other people's footsteps; nor does he gain entrance into the inner room either."[9]

走，学问道德也难以到家。”

21. 子曰：“论笃是与，君子者乎？色庄者乎？”

孔子说：“总是推许言论笃实的人，这种笃实的人是真正的君子呢？还是神情上伪装庄重的人呢？”

22. 子路问：“闻斯行诸？”子曰：“有父兄在，如之何其闻斯行之？”

冉有问：“闻斯行诸？”子曰：“闻斯行之。”

公西华曰：“由也问闻斯行诸，子曰，‘有父兄在’；求也问闻斯行诸，子曰，‘闻斯行之’。赤也惑，敢问。”

子曰：“求也退，故进之；由也兼人，故退之。”

子路问：“听到就干起来吗？”孔子道：“有爸爸哥哥活着，怎么能听到就干起来？”

冉有问：“听到就干起来吗？”孔子道：“听到就干起来。”

公西华道：“仲由问听到就干起来吗，您说：‘有爸爸哥哥活着，［不能这样做。］’冉求问听到就干起来吗，您说：‘听到就干起来。’［两个人问题相同，而您的答复相反，］我有些糊涂，大胆地来问问。”孔子道：“冉求平日做事退缩，所以我给他壮胆；仲由的胆量却有两个人的大，勇于作为，所以我要压压他。”

9. For the expression "inner room" see chapter 15 above.

21. The Master said, "Is one who simply sides with tenacious opinions a gentleman, or is he merely putting on a dignified appearance?"

22. Zi-lu asked, "Should one immediately put into practice what one has heard?" The Master said, "As your father and elder brothers are still alive, you are hardly in a position immediately to put into practice what you have heard."

Ran You asked, "Should one immediately put into practice what one has heard?" The Master said, "Yes. One should."

Gong-xi Hua said, "When You asked whether one should immediately put into practice what one had heard, you pointed out that his father and elder brothers were alive. Yet when Qiu asked whether one should immediately put into practice what one had heard, you answered that one should. I am puzzled. May I be enlightened?"

The Master said, "Qiu holds himself back. It is for this reason that I tried to urge him on. You has the drive of two men. It is for this reason that I tried to hold him back."

23. 子畏于匡，颜渊后。子曰：“吾以女为死矣。”

曰：“子在，回何敢死？”

孔子在匡被囚禁了之后，颜渊最后才来。孔子道：“我以为你是死了。”颜渊道：“您还活着，我怎么敢死呢？”

24. 季子然问：“仲由、冉求可谓大臣与？”

子曰：“吾以子为异之问，曾由与求之问。所谓大臣者，以道事君，不可则止。今由与求也，可谓具臣矣。”

曰：“然则从之者与？”

子曰：“弑父与君，亦不从也。”

季子然问：“仲由和冉求可以说是大臣吗？”孔子道：“我以为你是问别的人，竟问由和求呀。我们所说的大臣，他用最合于仁义的内容和方式来对待君主，如果这样行不通，宁肯辞职不干。如今由和求这两个人，可以说是具有相当才能的臣属了。”

季子然又道：“那么，他们会一切顺从上级吗？”孔子道：“杀父亲、杀君主的事情，他们也不会顺从的。”

25. 子路使子羔为费宰。子曰：“贼夫人之子。”

子路曰：“有民人焉，有社稷焉，何必读书，然后为学？”

子曰：“是故恶夫佞者。”

23. When the Master met with danger in Kuang, Yan Yuan fell behind. The Master said, "I thought you had met your death."

"While you, Master, are alive, how would I dare die?"

24. Ji Zi-Ran asked, "Can Zhong You and Ran Qiu be called great ministers?"

The Master said, "I had expected a somewhat different question. It never occurred to me that you were going to ask about You and Qiu. The term 'great minister' refers to those who serve their lord according to the Way and who, when this is no longer possible, relinquish office. Now men like You and Qiu can be described as ministers appointed to make up the full quota."

"In that case, are they the kind that will always do as they are told?"

"No. They will not do so when it comes to patricide or regicide."

25. On the occasion Zi-lu made Zi-gao the prefect of Bi, the Master said, "He is ruining another man's son."

Zi-lu said, "There are the common people and one's fellow

子路叫子羔去做费县县长。孔子道："这是害了别人的儿子！"

子路道："那地方有老百姓，有土地和五谷，为什么定要读书才叫做学问呢？"

孔子道："所以我讨厌强嘴利舌的人。"

26. 子路、曾皙、冉有、公西华侍坐。子曰："以吾一日长乎尔，毋吾以也。居则曰：'不吾知也！'如或知尔，则何以哉？"

子路率尔而对曰："千乘之国，摄乎大国之间，加之以师旅，因之以饥馑；由也为之，比及三年，可使有勇，且知方也。"

夫子哂之。

"求！尔何如？"

对曰："方六七十，如五六十，求也为之，比及三年，可使足民。如其礼乐，以俟君子。"

"赤！尔何如？"

对曰："非曰能之，愿学焉。宗庙之事，如会同，端章甫，愿为小相焉。"

"点！尔何如？"

鼓瑟希，铿尔，舍瑟而作，对曰："异乎三子者之撰。"

子曰："何伤乎？亦各言其志也。"

曰："莫春者，春服既成，冠者五六人，童子六七人，浴

men, and there are the altars to the gods of earth and grain. Why must one have to read books before one is said to learn?"

The Master said, "It is for this reason that I dislike men who are plausible."

26. When Zi-lu, Zeng Xi, Ran You and Gong-xi Hua were seated in attendance, the Master said, "Do not feel constrained simply because I am somewhat older than you are. Now you are in the habit of saying, 'My abilities are not appreciated,' but if someone did appreciate your abilities, do tell me how you would go about things."

Zi-lu promptly answered, "If I were to administer a state of a thousand chariots, situated between powerful neighbours, troubled by armed invasions and by repeated famines, I could, within three years, give the people courage and a sense of direction."

The Master smiled at him.

"Qiu, what about you?"

"If I were to administer an area measuring sixty or seventy *li* square, or even fifty or sixty *li* square, I could, within three

乎沂，风乎舞雩，咏而归。”

夫子喟然叹曰：“吾与点也!”

三子者出，曾皙后。曾皙曰：“夫三子者之言何如?”

子曰：“亦各言其志也已矣。”

曰：“夫子何哂由也?”

曰：“为国以礼，其言不让，是故哂之。”

“唯求则非邦也与?”

“安见方六七十如五六十而非邦也者?”

“唯赤则非邦也与?”

“宗庙会同，非诸侯而何?赤也为之小，孰能为之大?”

子路、曾皙、冉有、公西华四个人陪着孔子坐着。

孔子说道:“因为我比你们年纪都大，[老了,] 没有人用我了。你们平日说:‘人家不了解我呀!’假若有人了解你们，[打算请你们出去,] 那你们怎么办呢?”

子路不加思索地答道:“一千辆兵车的国家，局促地处于几个大国的中间，外面有军队侵犯它，国内又加以灾荒。我去治理，等到三年光景，可以使人人有勇气，而且懂得大道理。”

孔子微微一笑。

又问:“冉求！你怎么样?”

答道:“国土纵横各六七十里或者五六十里的小国家，我

years, bring the size of the population up to an adequate level. As to the rites and music, I would leave that to abler gentlemen."

"Chi, how about you?"

"I do not say that I already have the ability, but I am ready to learn. On ceremonial occasions in the ancestral temple or in diplomatic gatherings, I should like to assist as a minor official in charge of protocol, properly dressed in my ceremonial cap and robes."

"Dian, how about you?"

After strumming a few dying notes and the final chord, he stood up from his lute. "I differ from the other three in my choice."

The Master said, "What harm is there in that? After all each man is stating what he has set his heart upon."

"In late spring, after the spring clothes have been newly made, I should like, together with five or six adults and six or seven boys, to go bathing in the River Yi and enjoy the breeze on the Rain Altar, and then to go home chanting poetry."

The Master sighed and said, "I am all in favour of Dian."

When the three left, Zeng Xi stayed behind. He said,

去治理，等到三年光景，可以使人人富足。至于修明礼乐，那只有等待贤人君子了。”

又问：“公西赤！你怎么样？”

答道：“不是说我已经很有本领了，我愿意这样学习：祭祀的工作或者同外国盟会，我愿意穿着礼服，戴着礼帽，做一个小司仪者。”

又问：“曾点！你怎么样？”

他弹瑟正近尾声，铿的一声把瑟放下，站了起来答道：“我的志向和他们三位所讲的不同。”

孔子道：“那有什么妨碍呢？正是要各人说出自己的志向啊！”

曾晳便道：“暮春三月，春天衣服都穿定了，我陪同五六位成年人，六七个小孩，在沂水旁边洗洗澡，在舞雩台上吹吹风，一路唱歌，一路走回来。”

孔子长叹一声道：“我同意曾点的主张呀！”

子路、冉有、公西华三人都出来了，曾晳后走。曾晳问道：“那三位同学的话怎样？”

孔子道：“也不过各人说说自己的志向罢了。”

曾晳又道：“您为什么对仲由微笑呢？”

孔子道：“治理国家应该讲求礼让，可是他的话却一点不谦虚，所以笑笑他。”

“难道冉求所讲的就不是国家吗？”

"What do you think of what the other three said?"

"They were only stating what they had set their hearts up-on."

"Why did you smile at You?"

"It is by the rites that a state is administered, but in the way he spoke You showed a lack of modesty. That is why I smiled at him."

"In the case of Qiu, was he not concerned with a state?"

"What can justify one in saying that sixty or seventy *li* square or indeed fifty or sixty *li* square do not deserve the name of 'state'?"

"In the case of Chi, was he not concerned with a state?"

"What are ceremonial occasions in the ancestral temple and diplomatic gatherings if not matters which concern rulers of feudal states? If Chi plays only a minor part, who would be able to play a major role?"

先进篇第十一

孔子道："怎样见得纵横各六七十里或者五六十里的土地就不够是一个国家呢？"

"公西赤所讲的不是国家吗？"

孔子道："有宗庙，有国际间的盟会，不是国家是什么？[我笑仲由的不是说他不能治理国家，关键不在是不是国家，而是笑他说话的内容和态度不够谦虚。譬如公西赤，他是个十分懂得礼仪的人，但他只说愿意学着做一个小司仪者。] 如果他只做一个小司仪者，又有谁来做大司仪者呢？"

BOOK 11

颜渊篇第十二

1. 颜渊问仁。子曰："克己复礼为仁。一日克己复礼，天下归仁焉。为仁由己，而由人乎哉？"

颜渊曰："请问其目。"子曰："非礼勿视，非礼勿听，非礼勿言，非礼勿动。"

颜渊曰："回虽不敏，请事斯语矣。"

颜渊问仁德。孔子道："抑制自己，使言语行动都合于礼，就是仁。一旦这样做到了，天下的人都会称许你是仁人。实践仁德，全凭自己，还凭别人吗？"

颜渊道："请问行动的纲领。"孔子道："不合礼的事不看，不合礼的话不听，不合礼的话不说，不合礼的事不做。"

颜渊道："我虽然迟钝，也要实行您这话。"

2. 仲弓问仁。子曰："出门如见大宾，使民如承大祭。己所不欲，勿施于人。在邦无怨，在家无怨。"

仲弓曰："雍虽不敏，请事斯语矣。"

仲弓问仁德。孔子道："出门［工作］好像去接待贵宾，役使百姓好像去承当大祀典，［都得严肃认真，小心谨慎。］自己所不喜欢的事物，就不强加于别人。在工作岗位上不对

BOOK 12

1. Yan Yuan asked about benevolence. The Master said, "To return to the observance of the rites through overcoming the self constitutes benevolence. If for a single day a man could return to the observance of the rites through overcoming himself, then the whole Empire would consider benevolence to be his. However, the practice of benevolence depends on oneself alone, and not on others."

Yan Yuan said, "I should like you to list the items."

The Master said, "Do not look unless it is in accordance with the rites; do not listen unless it is in accordance with the rites; do not speak unless it is in accordance with the rites; do not move unless it is in accordance with the rites."

Yan Yuan said, "Though I am not quick, I shall direct my efforts towards what you have said."

2. Zhong-gong asked about benevolence. The Master said, "When abroad behave as though you were receiving an important guest. When employing the services of the common people behave as though you were officiating at an important sacrifice. Do not impose on others what you yourself do not desire.[1] In this way you will be free from ill will whether in a state or in a

工作有怨恨，就是不在工作岗位上也没有怨恨。”

仲弓道：“我虽然迟钝，也要实行您这话。”

3. 司马牛问仁。子曰：“仁者，其言也讱。”

曰：“其言也讱，斯谓之仁已乎？”

子曰：“为之难，言之得无讱乎？”

司马牛问仁德。孔子道：“仁人，他的言语迟钝。”

司马牛道：“言语迟钝，这就叫做仁了吗？”孔子道：“做起来不容易，说话能够不迟钝吗？”

4. 司马牛问君子。子曰：“君子不忧不惧。”

曰：“不忧不惧，斯谓之君子已乎？”

子曰：“内省不疚，夫何忧何惧？”

司马牛问怎样去做一个君子。孔子道：“君子不忧愁，不恐惧。”

司马牛道：“不忧愁，不恐惧，这样就可以叫做君子了吗？”孔子道：“自己问心无愧，那有什么可以忧愁和恐惧的呢？”

noble family."

Zhong-gong said, "Though I am not quick, I shall direct my efforts towards what you have said."

1. This sentence is to be found in XV.24.

3. Si-ma Niu asked about benevolence. The Master said, "The mark of the benevolent man is that he is loath to speak."

"In that case, can a man be said to be benevolent simply because he is loath to speak?"

The Master said, "When to act is difficult, is it any wonder that one is loath to speak?"[2]

2. for fear that one may be unable to live up to one's words. Cf. IV.22, IV.24.

4. Si-ma Niu asked about the gentleman. The Master said, "The gentleman is free from worries and fears."

"In that case, can a man be said to be a gentleman simply because he is free from worries and fears?"

The Master said, "If, upon self-examination, a man finds nothing to reproach himself for, what worries and fears can he have?"

5. 司马牛忧曰："人皆有兄弟，我独亡。"

子夏曰："商闻之矣：死生有命，富贵在天。君子敬而无失，与人恭而有礼。四海之内，皆兄弟也——君子何患乎无兄弟也？"

司马牛忧愁地说道："别人都有好兄弟，单单我没有。"子夏道："我听说过：死生听之命运，富贵由天安排。君子只是对待工作严肃认真，不出差错，对待别人词色恭谨，合乎礼节，天下之大，到处都是好兄弟——君子又何必着急没有好兄弟呢？"

6. 子张问明。子曰："浸润之谮，肤受之愬，不行焉，可谓明也已矣。浸润之谮，肤受之愬，不行焉，可谓远也已矣。"

子张问怎样才叫做见事明白。孔子道："点滴而来、日积月累的谗言和肌肤所受、急迫切身的诬告都在你这里行不通，那你可以说是看得明白的了。点滴而来、日积月累的谗言和肌肤所受、急迫切身的诬告也都在你这里行不通，那你可以说是看得远的了。"

7. 子贡问政。子曰："足食，足兵，民信之矣。"

子贡曰："必不得已而去，于斯三者何先？"

曰："去兵。"

BOOK 12

5. Si-ma Niu appeared worried, saying, "All men have brothers. I alone have none."

Zi-xia said, "I have heard it said: life and death are a matter of Destiny; wealth and honour depend on Heaven. The gentleman is reverent and does nothing amiss, is respectful towards others and observant of the rites, and all within the Four Seas are his brothers. What need is there for the gentleman to worry about not having any brothers?"

6. Zi-zhang asked about perspicacity. The Master said, "When a man is not influenced by slanders which are assiduously repeated or by complaints for which he feels a direct sympathy, he can be said to be perspicacious. He can at the same time be said to be far-sighted."

7. Zi-gong asked about government. The Master said, "Give them enough food, give them enough arms, and the common people will have trust in you."

子贡曰："必不得已而去，于斯二者何先？"

曰："去食。自古皆有死，民无信不立。"

子贡问怎样去治理政事。孔子道："充足粮食，充足军备，百姓对政府就有信心了。"

子贡道："如果迫于不得已，在粮食、军备和人民的信心三者之中一定要去掉一项，先去掉哪一项？"孔子道："去掉军备。"

子贡道："如果迫于不得已，在粮食和人民的信心两者之中一定要去掉一项，先去掉哪一项？"孔子道："去掉粮食。[没有粮食，不过死亡，但] 自古以来谁都免不了死亡。如果人民对政府缺乏信心，国家是站不起来的。"

8. 棘子成曰："君子质而已矣，何以文为？"

子贡曰："惜乎，夫子之说君子也！驷不及舌。文犹质也，质犹文也。虎豹之鞟犹犬羊之鞟。"

棘子成道："君子只要有好的本质便够了，要那些文彩 [那些仪节、那些形式] 干什么？"子贡道："先生这样地谈论君子，可惜说错了。一言既出，驷马难追。本质和文彩，是同等重要的。假若把虎豹和犬羊两类兽皮拔去有文彩的毛，那这两类皮革就很少区别了。"

Zi-gong said, "If one had to give up one of these three, which should one give up first?"

"Give up arms."

Zi-gong said, "If one had to give up one of the remaining two, which should one give up first?"

"Give up food. Death has always been with us since the beginning of time, but when there is no trust, the common people will not be able to stand on their feet."

8. Ji Zi-cheng said, "The important thing about the gentleman is the stuff he is made of. What does he need refinement for?" Zi-gong commented, "It is a pity that this gentleman should have spoken so about the gentleman, for 'a team of horses cannot catch up with one's tongue.'[3] The stuff is no different from refinement; refinement is no different from the stuff. The pelt of a tiger or a leopard, shorn of hair, is no different from that of a dog or a sheep."

3. in other words, words once spoken cannot be recalled.

颜渊篇第十二

9. 哀公问于有若曰："年饥，用不足，如之何？"

有若对曰："盍彻乎？"

曰："二，吾犹不足，如之何其彻也？"

对曰："百姓足，君孰与不足？百姓不足，君孰与足？"

鲁哀公向有若问道："年成不好，国家用度不够，应该怎么办？"

有若答道："为什么不实行十分抽一的税率呢？"

哀公道："十分抽二，我还不够，怎么能十分抽一呢？"

答道："如果百姓的用度够，您怎么会不够？如果百姓的用度不够，您又怎么会够？"

10. 子张问崇德辨惑。子曰："主忠信，徙义，崇德也。爱之欲其生，恶之欲其死。既欲其生，又欲其死，是惑也。

'诚不以富，亦只以异。'"

子张问如何去提高品德，辨别迷惑。孔子道："以忠诚信实为主，唯义是从，这就可以提高品德。爱一个人，希望他长寿；厌恶起来，恨不得他马上死去。既要他长寿，又要他短命，这便是迷惑。这样，的确对自己毫无好处，只是使人奇怪罢了。"

BOOK 12

9. Duke Ai asked You Ruo, "The harvest is bad, and I have not sufficient to cover expenditure. What should I do?"

You Ruo answered, "What about taxing the people one part in ten?"

"I do not have sufficient as it is when I tax them two parts in ten. How could I possibly tax them one part in ten?"

"When the people have sufficient, who is there to share your insufficiency? When the people have insufficient, who is there to share your sufficiency?"

10. Zi-zhang asked about the exaltation of virtue and the resolution of perplexities. The Master said, "Make it your guiding principle to do your best for others and to be trustworthy in what you say, and move yourself to where rightness is, then you will be exalting virtue. When you love a man you want him to live and when you hate him you want him to die. If, wanting him to live, you also want him to die, is this not being perplexed.

If you did not do so for the sake of riches,

You must have done so for the sake of novelty."[4]

4. The quotation which is from Ode 188 seems to have no bearing on the

颜渊篇第十二

11. 齐景公问政于孔子。孔子对曰："君君，臣臣，父父，子子。"

公曰："善哉！信如君不君，臣不臣，父不父，子不子，虽有粟，吾得而食诸？"

齐景公向孔子问政治。孔子答道："君要像个君，臣要像个臣，父亲要像父亲，儿子要像儿子。"景公道："对呀！若是君不像君，臣不像臣，父不像父，子不像子，即使粮食很多，我能吃得着吗？"

12. 子曰："片言可以折狱者，其由也与？"

子路无宿诺。

孔子说："根据一方面的语言就可以判决案件的，大概只有仲由吧！"

子路从不拖延诺言。

13. 子曰："听讼，吾犹人也。必也使无讼乎！"

孔子说："审理诉讼，我同别人差不多。一定要使诉讼的事件完全消灭才好。"

subject under discussion. It has been suggested that it does not belong here.

11. Duke Jing of Qi asked Confucius about government. Confucius answered, "Let the ruler be a ruler, the subject a subject, the father a father, the son a son."

The Duke said, "Splendid! Truly, if the ruler be not a ruler, the subject not a subject, the father not a father, the son not a son, then even if there be grain, would I get to eat it?"

12. The Master said, "If anyone can arrive at the truth in a legal dispute on the evidence of only one party, it is, perhaps, You."

Zi-lu never put off the fulfilment of a promise to the next day.

13. The Master said, "In hearing litigation, I am no different from any other man. But if you insist on a difference, it is, perhaps, that I try to get the parties not to resort to litigation in the first place."

颜渊篇第十二

14. 子张问政。子曰："居之无倦，行之以忠。"

子张问政治。孔子道："在位不要疲倦懈怠，执行政令要忠心。"

15. 子曰："博学于文，约之以礼，亦可以弗畔矣夫！"

16. 子曰："君子成人之美，不成人之恶，小人反是。"

孔子说："君子成全别人的好事，不促成别人的坏事。小人却和这相反。"

17. 季康子问政于孔子。孔子对曰："政者，正也。子帅以正，孰敢不正？"

季康子向孔子问政治。孔子答道："政字的意思就是端正。您自己带头端正，谁敢不端正呢？"

18. 季康子患盗，问于孔子。孔子对曰："苟子之不欲，虽赏之不

14. Zi–zhang asked about government. The Master said, "In the daily round do not show weariness, and when there is action to be taken, do your best."

15. The Master said, "Being widely versed in culture but brought back to essentials by the rites a man can, I suppose, be relied upon not to turn against what he stood for."[5]

5. This is a repetition of VI.27.

16. The Master said, "The gentleman helps others to effect what is good; he does not help them to effect what is bad. The small man does the opposite."

17. Ji Kang Zi asked Confucius about government. Confucius answered, "Government (*zheng*) is being correct (*zheng*).[6] If you give a lead in being correct, who would dare to be incorrect?"

6. Besides being homophones, the two words in Chinese are cognate, thus showing that the concept of "government" was felt to be related to that of "being correct".

18. Troubled by thieves in the state, Ji Kang Zi asked the advice of

窃。”

季康子苦于盗贼太多，向孔子求教。孔子答道：“假若您不贪求太多的财货，就是奖励偷抢，他们也不会干。”

19. 季康子问政于孔子曰：“如杀无道，以就有道，何如?”

孔子对曰：“子为政，焉用杀?子欲善而民善矣。君子之德风，小人之德草。草上之风，必偃。”

季康子向孔子请教政治，说道：“假若杀掉坏人来亲近好人，怎么样?”孔子答道：“您治理政治，为什么要杀戮？您想把国家搞好，百姓就会好起来。领导人的作风好比风，老百姓的作风好比草。风向哪边吹，草向哪边倒。”

20. 子张问：“士何如斯可谓之达矣?”

子曰：“何哉，尔所谓达者?”

子张对曰：“在邦必闻，在家必闻。”

子曰：“是闻也，非达也。夫达也者，质直而好义，察言而观色，虑以下人。在邦必达，在家必达。夫闻也者，色取仁而行违，居之不疑。在邦必闻，在家必闻。”

Confucius who said, "If you yourself were a man of few desires,[7] no one would steal even if stealing carried a reward with it."

7. in other words, if you did not set an example by stealing from the people.

19. Ji Kang Zi asked Confucius about government, saying, "What would you think if, in order to move closer to those who possess the Way, I were to kill those who do not follow the Way?"

Confucius answered, "In administering your government, what need is there for you to kill? Just desire the good yourself and the common people will be good. By nature the gentleman is like wind and the small man like grass. Let the wind sweep over the grass and it is sure to bend."[8]

8. This saying is quoted in the Mencius, III.A.2.

20. Zi-zhang asked, "What must a Gentleman be like before he can be said to have got through?"

The Master said, "What on earth do you mean by getting through?"

Zi-zhang answered, "What I have in mind is a man who is sure to be known whether he serves in a state or in a noble

子张问："读书人要怎样做才可以叫达了？"孔子道："你所说的达是什么意思？"子张答道："做国家的官时一定有名望，在大夫家工作时一定有名望。"孔子道："这个叫闻，不叫达。怎样才是达呢？品质正直，遇事讲理，善于分析别人的言语，观察别人的颜色，从思想上愿意对别人退让。这种人，做国家的官时固然事事行得通，在大夫家一定事事行得通。至于闻，表面上似乎爱好仁德，实际行为却不如此，可是自己竟以仁人自居而不加疑惑。这种人，做官的时候一定会骗取名望，居家的时候也一定会骗取名望。"

21. 樊迟从游于舞雩之下，曰："敢问崇德，修慝，辨惑。"

子曰："善哉问！先事后得，非崇德与？攻其恶，无攻人之恶，非修慝与？一朝之忿，忘其身，以及其亲，非惑与？"

樊迟陪侍孔子在舞雩台下游逛，说道："请问怎样提高自己的品德，怎样消除别人对自己不露面的怨恨，怎样辨别出哪种是糊涂事。"孔子道："问得好！首先付出劳动，然后收获，不是提高品德了吗？批判自己的坏处，不去批判别人的坏处，不就消除无形的怨恨了吗？因为偶然的忿怒，便忘记

family."

The Master said, "That is being known, not getting through. Now the term 'getting through' describes a man who is straight by nature and fond of what is right, sensitive to other people's words and observant of the expression on their faces, and always mindful of being modest. Such a man is bound to get through whether he serves in a state or in a noble family. On the other hand, the term 'being known' describes a man who has no misgivings about his own claim to benevolence when all he is doing is putting up a facade of benevolence which is belied by his deeds. Such a man is sure to be known, whether he serves in a state or in a noble family."

21. Fan Chi was in attendance during an outing to the Rain Altar. He said, "May I ask about the exaltation of virtue, the reformation of the depraved and the resolution of perplexities?"

The Master said, "What a splendid question! To put service before the reward you get for it, is that not exaltation of virtue?[9] To attack evil as evil and not as evil of a particular man, is that not the way to reform the depraved? To let a sudden fit of anger make you forget the safety of your own person or even

自己，甚至也忘记了爹娘，不是糊涂吗？”

22. 樊迟问仁。子曰：“爱人。”

问知。子曰：“知人。”樊迟未达。子曰：“举直错诸枉，能使枉者直。”

樊迟退，见子夏曰：“乡也吾见于夫子而问知，子曰，‘举直错诸枉，能使枉者直’，何谓也？”

子夏曰：“富哉言乎！舜有天下，选于众，举皋陶，不仁者远矣。汤有天下，选于众，举伊尹，不仁者远矣。”

樊迟问仁。孔子道：“爱人。”又问智。孔子道：“善于鉴别人物。”

樊迟还不透彻了解。孔子道：“把正直人提拔出来，位置在邪恶人之上，能够使邪恶人正直。”

樊迟退了出来，找着子夏，说道：“刚才我去见老师向他问智，他说，‘把正直人提拔出来，位置在邪恶人之上’，这是什么意思？”

子夏道：“意义多么丰富的话呀！舜有了天下，在众人之中挑选，把皋陶提拔出来，坏人就难以存在了。汤有了天下，在众人之中挑选，把伊尹提拔出来，坏人也就难以存在了。”

that of your parents, is that not being perplexed?"

9. The two words *de* 得 (to get) and *de* 德 (virtue) seem to be cognate. Virtue is what one makes one's own by the pursuit of the *dao* (Way).

22. Fan Chi asked about benevolence. The Master said, "Love your fellow men."

He asked about wisdom. The Master said, "Know your fellow men." Fan Chi failed to grasp his meaning. The Master said, "Raise the straight and set them over the crooked. [10] This can make the crooked straight."

Fan Chi withdrew and went to see Zi-xia, saying, "Just now, I went to see the Master and asked about wisdom. The Master said, 'Raise the straight and set them over the crooked. This can make the crooked straight.' What did he mean?"

Zi-xia said, "Rich, indeed, is the meaning of these words. When Shun possessed the Empire, he raised Gao Yao from the multitude and by so doing placed those who were not benevolent at a great distance. When Tang possessed the Empire, he raised Yi Yin from the multitude and by so doing placed those who were not benevolent at a great distance."

10. For this saying see II. 19.

颜渊篇第十二

23. 子贡问友。子曰："忠告而善道之，不可则止，毋自辱焉。"

子贡问对待朋友的方法。孔子道："忠心地劝告他，好好地引导他，他不听从，也就罢了，不要自找侮辱。"

24. 曾子曰："君子以文会友，以友辅仁。"

曾子说："君子用文章学问来聚会朋友，用朋友来帮助我培养仁德。"

23. Zi-gong asked about how friends should be treated. The Master said, "Advise them to the best of your ability and guide them properly, but stop when there is no hope of success. Do not ask to be snubbed."[11]

11. Cf. IV.26.

24. Zeng Zi said, "A gentleman makes friends through being cultivated, but looks to friends for support in benevolence."

子路篇第十三

1. 子路问政。子曰："先之劳之。"请益。曰："无倦。"

子路问政治。孔子道："自己给百姓带头，然后让他们勤劳地工作。"子路请求多讲一点。孔子又道："永远不要懈怠。"

2. 仲弓为季氏宰，问政。子曰："先有司，赦小过，举贤才。"

曰："焉知贤才而举之？"

子曰："举尔所知；尔所不知，人其舍诸？"

仲弓做了季氏的总管，向孔子问政治。孔子道："给工作人员带头，不计较人家的小错误，提拔优秀人才。"

仲弓道："怎样去识别优秀人才把他们提拔出来呢？"孔子道："提拔你所知道的；那些你所不知道的，别人难道会埋没他吗？"

3. 子路曰："卫君待子而为政，子将奚先？"

子曰："必也正名乎！"

子路曰："有是哉，子之迂也！奚其正？"

子曰："野哉，由也！君子于其所不知，盖阙如也。名不正，则言不顺；言不顺，则事不成；事不成，则礼乐不兴；礼乐不兴，则刑罚不中；刑罚不中，则民无所错手足。故君子名之必可言也，言之必可行也。君子于其言，无所苟而已矣。"

BOOK 13

1. Zi–lu asked about government. The Master said, "Before working the people hard first set an example yourself." Zi–lu asked for more. The Master said, "Do not allow your efforts to slacken."

2. While he was steward to the Ji family, Zhong–gong asked about government. The Master said, "Set an example for your officials to follow; show leniency towards minor offenders; and promote men of talent."

"How does one recognize men of talent to promote?"

"Promote those you do recognize. Do you suppose others will allow those you fail to recognize to be passed over?"

3. Zi–lu said, "If the Lord of Wei left the administration (*zheng*) of his state to you, what would you put first?"

The Master said, "If something has to be put first, it is, perhaps, the rectification (*zheng*)[1] of names."

Zi–lu said, "How extraordinary the roundabout way you take! Why bring rectification in at all?"

The Master said, "You, how boorish you are. Where a gen–

子路篇第十三

子路对孔子说："卫君等着您去治理国政，您准备首先干什么？"

孔子道："那一定是纠正名分上的用词不当罢！"

子路道："您的迂腐竟到如此地步吗！这又何必纠正？"

孔子道："你怎么这样卤莽！君子对于他所不懂的，大概采取保留态度，［你怎么能乱说呢？］用词不当，言语就不能顺理成章；言语不顺理成章，工作就不可能搞好；工作搞不好，国家的礼乐制度也就举办不起来；礼乐制度举办不起来，刑罚也就不会得当；刑罚不得当，百姓就会［惶惶不安，］连手脚都不晓得摆在哪里才好。所以君子用一个词，一定［有它一定的理由，］可以说得出来；而顺理成章的话也一定行得通。君子对于措词说话要没有一点马虎的地方才罢了。"

4. 樊迟请学稼。子曰："吾不如老农。"请学为圃。曰："吾不如老圃。"

樊迟出。子曰："小人哉，樊须也！上好礼，则民莫敢不敬；上好义，则民莫敢不服；上好信，则民莫敢不用情。夫如是，则四方之民襁负其子而至矣，焉用稼？"

樊迟请求学种庄稼。孔子道："我不如老农民。"又请求学

tleman is ignorant, one would expect him not to offer any opinion. When names are not correct, what is said will not sound reasonable; when what is said does not sound reasonable, affairs will not culminate in success; when affairs do not culminate in success, rites and music will not flourish; when rites and music do not flourish, punishments will not be exactly right; when punishments are not exactly right, the common people will not know where to put hand and foot. Thus when the gentleman names something, the name is sure to be usable in speech, and when he says something this is sure to be practicable. The thing about the gentleman is that he is anything but casual where speech is concerned."

1. For a discussion about the two words pronounced *zheng* see note to XII. 17.

4. Fan Chi asked to be taught how to grow crops. The Master said, "I am not as good as an old farmer." He asked to be taught how to grow vegetables. "I am not as good as an old gardener."

When Fan Chi left, the Master said, "How petty Fan Xu is! When those above love the rites, none of the common

种菜蔬。孔子道:“我不如老菜农。”

樊迟退了出来。孔子道:“樊迟真是小人!统治者讲究礼节,百姓就没有人敢不尊敬;统治者行为正当,百姓就没有人敢不服从;统治者诚恳信实,百姓就没有人敢不说真话。做到这样,四方的百姓都会背负着小儿女来投奔,为什么要自己种庄稼呢?”

5. 子曰:“诵《诗》三百,授之以政,不达;使于四方,不能专对;虽多,亦奚以为?”

孔子说:“熟读《诗经》三百篇,交给他以政治任务,却办不通;叫他出使外国,又不能独立地去谈判酬酢;纵是读得多,有什么用处呢?”

6. 子曰:“其身正,不令而行;其身不正,虽令不从。”

孔子说:“统治者本身行为正当,不发命令,事情也行得通。他本身行为不正当,纵三令五申,百姓也不会信从。”

7. 子曰:“鲁卫之政,兄弟也。”

孔子说:“鲁国的政治和卫国的政治,像兄弟一般[地相

people will dare be irreverent; when they love what is right, none of the common people will dare not to submit; when they love trustworthiness, none of the common people will dare not to show their true colours. In this way, the common people from the four quarters will come with their children strapped on their backs. What need is there to talk about growing crops?"

5. The Master said, "If a man who knows the three hundred pieces in the *Odes* by heart fails when given administrative responsibilities and proves incapable of exercising his own initiative when sent to foreign states, then what use are these to him, however many they may be?"

6. The Master said, "If a man is correct in his own person, then there will be obedience without orders being given; but if he is not correct in his own person, there will not be obedience even though orders are given."

7. The Master said, "In their government the states of Lu and Wei are as alike as brothers."

差不远]。”

8. 子谓卫公子荆，“善居室。始有，曰：‘苟合矣。’少有，曰：‘苟完矣。’富有，曰：‘苟美矣。’”

孔子谈到卫国的公子荆，说：“他善于居家过日子，刚有一点，便说道：‘差不多够了。’增加了一点，又说道：‘差不多完备了。’多有一点，便说道：‘差不多富丽堂皇了。’”

9. 子适卫，冉有仆。子曰：“庶矣哉！”

冉有曰：“既庶矣，又何加焉？”

曰：“富之。”

曰：“既富矣，又何加焉？”

曰：“教之。”

孔子到卫国，冉有替他驾车子。孔子道：“好稠密的人口！”

冉有道：“人口已经众多了，又该怎么办呢？”孔子道：“使他们富裕起来。”

冉有道：“已经富裕了，又该怎么办呢？”孔子道：“教育他们。”

10. 子曰：“苟有用我者，期月而已可也，三年有成。”

BOOK 13

8. The Master said about Prince Jing of Wei that he showed a laudable attitude towards a house as a place to live in. When he first had a house, he said, "It is more or less adequate." When he had extended it somewhat, he said, "It has more or less everything." When it had become sumptuous, he said, "It is more or less grand enough."

9. When the Master went to Wei, Ran You drove for him. The Master said, "What a teeming population!"

Ran You said, "When the population is teeming, what further benefit can one add?"

"Improve their circumstances."

"When their circumstances have been improved, what further benefit can one add?"

"*Train them.*"[2]

2. For the training of the people see chapters 29 and 30 below.

10. The Master said, "If anyone were to employ me, in a year's

孔子说："假若有用我主持国家政事的，一年便差不多了，三年便会很有成绩。"

11. 子曰："'善人为邦百年，亦可以胜残去杀矣。'诚哉是言也！"

孔子说："'善人治理国政连续到一百年，也可以克服残暴免除虐杀了。'这句话真说得对呀！"

12. 子曰："如有王者，必世而后仁。"

孔子说："假若有王者兴起，一定需要三十年才能使仁政大行。"

13. 子曰："苟正其身矣，于从政乎何有？不能正其身，如正人何？"

孔子说："假若端正了自己，治理国政有什么困难呢？连本身都不能端正，怎么端正别人呢？"

14. 冉子退朝。子曰："何晏也？"

对曰："有政。"

子曰："其事也。如有政，虽不吾以，吾其与闻之。"

冉有从办公的地方回来。孔子道："为什么今天回得这样

time I would have brought things to a satisfactory state, and after three years I should have results to show for it."

11. The Master said, "How true is the saying that after a state has been ruled for a hundred years by good men it is possible to get the better of cruelty and to do away with killing."

12. The Master said, "Even with a true king it is bound to take a generation for benevolence to become a reality."

13. The Master said, "If a man manages to make himself correct, what is there to taking office for him? If he cannot make himself correct, what business has he with making others correct?"[3]

3. For the connection between government and correction see XII. 17.

14. Ran Zi returned from court. The Master said, "Why so late?"

"There were affairs of state."

The Master said, "They could only have been routine matters. Were there affairs of state, I would get to hear of them,

晚呢？”答道：“有政务。”孔子道：“那只是事务罢了。若是有政务，虽然不用我了，我也会知道的。”

15. 定公问：“一言而可以兴邦，有诸？”

孔子对曰：“言不可以若是其几也。人之言曰：‘为君难，为臣不易。’如知为君之难也，不几乎一言而兴邦乎？”

曰：“一言而丧邦，有诸？”

孔子对曰：“言不可以若是其几也。人之言曰：‘予无乐乎为君，唯其言而莫予违也。’如其善而莫之违也，不亦善乎？如不善而莫之违也，不几乎一言而丧邦乎？”

鲁定公问：“一句话兴盛国家，有这事么？”

孔子答道：“说话不可以像这样地简单机械。不过，大家都说：‘做君上很难，做臣子不容易。’假若知道做君上的艰难，［自然会谨慎认真地干去，］不近于一句话便兴盛国家么？”

定公又道：“一句话丧失国家，有这事么？”

孔子答道：“说话不可以像这样地简单机械。不过，大家都说：‘我做国君没有别的快乐，只是我说什么话都没有人违抗我。’假若说的话正确而没有人违抗，不也好么？假若说的话不正确而也没有人违抗，不近于一句话便丧失国家么？”

even though I am no longer actively employed."

15. Duke Ding asked, "Is there such a thing as a single saying that can make a state prosper?"

Confucius answered, "A saying cannot quite do that. There is a saying amongst men: 'It is difficult to be a ruler, and it is not easy to be a subject either.' If the ruler understands the difficulty of being a ruler, then is this not almost a case of a saying making a state prosper?"

"Is there such a thing as a saying that can ruin a state?"

Confucius answered, "A saying cannot quite do that. There is a saying amongst men: 'I do not at all enjoy being a ruler, except for the fact that there is no one to go against what I say.' If what he says is good and no one goes against him, good. But if what he says is not good and no one goes against him, then is this not almost a case of a saying ruining a state?"

子路篇第十三

16. 叶公问政。子曰："近者悦，远者来。"

叶公问政治。孔子道："境内的人使他高兴，境外的人使他来投奔。"

17. 子夏为莒父宰，问政。子曰："无欲速，无见小利。欲速，则不达；见小利，则大事不成。"

子夏做了莒父的县长，问政治。孔子道："不要图快，不要顾小利。图快，反而不能达到目的；顾小利，就办不成大事。"

18. 叶公语孔子曰："吾党有直躬者，其父攘羊，而子证之。"

孔子曰："吾党之直者异于是:父为子隐，子为父隐。——直在其中矣。"

叶公告诉孔子道："我那里有个坦白直率的人，他父亲偷了羊，他便告发。"孔子道："我们那里坦白直率的人和你们的不同:父亲替儿子隐瞒，儿子替父亲隐瞒——直率就在这里面。"

19. 樊迟问仁。子曰："居处恭，执事敬，与人忠。虽之夷狄，不可弃也。"

16. The Governor of She asked about government. The Master said, "Ensure that those who are near are pleased and those who are far away are attracted."

17. On becoming prefect of Ju Fu, Zi-xia asked about government. The Master said, "Do not be impatient. Do not see only petty gains. If you are impatient, you will not reach your goal. If you see only petty gains, the great tasks will not be accomplished."

18. The Governor of She said to Confucius, "In our village we have one Straight Body. When his father stole a sheep, he the son gave evidence against him."

Confucius answered, "In our village those who are straight are quite different. Fathers cover up for their sons, and sons cover up for their fathers. In such behaviour is straightness to be found as a matter of course."

19. Fan Chi asked about benevolence. The Master said, "While at home hold yourself in a respectful attitude; when serving in an official capacity be reverent; when dealing with others give of

樊迟问仁。孔子道："平日容貌态度端正庄严，工作严肃认真，为别人忠心诚意。这几种品德，纵到外国去，也是不能废弃的。"

20. 子贡问曰："何如斯可谓之士矣？"

子曰："行己有耻，使于四方，不辱君命，可谓士矣。"

曰："敢问其次。"

曰："宗族称孝焉，乡党称弟焉。"

曰："敢问其次。"

曰："言必信，行必果，硁硁然小人哉！——抑亦可以为次矣。"

曰："今之从政者何如？"子曰："噫！斗筲之人，何足算也？"

子贡问道："怎样才可以叫做'士'？"孔子道："自己行为保持羞耻之心，出使外国，很好地完成君主的使命，可以叫做'士'了。"

子贡道："请问次一等的。"孔子道："宗族称赞他孝顺父母，乡里称赞他恭敬尊长。"

子贡又道："请问再次一等的。"孔子道："言语一定信实，行为一定坚决，这是不问是非黑白而只管自己贯彻言行的小人呀！但也可以说是再次一等的'士'了。"

your best. These are qualities that cannot be put aside, even if you go and live among the barbarians."

20. Zi-gong asked, "What must a man be like before he can be said truly to be a Gentleman?"

The Master said, "A man who has a sense of shame in the way he conducts himself and, when sent abroad, does not disgrace the commission of his lord can be said to be a Gentleman."

"May I ask about the grade below?"

"Someone praised for being a good son in his clan and for being a respectful young man in the village."

"And the next?"

"A man who insists on keeping his word and seeing his actions through to the end can, perhaps, qualify to come next, even though he shows a stubborn petty-mindedness."

"What about men who are in public life in the present day?"

The Master said, "Oh, they are of such limited capacity that they hardly count."

子贡道："现在的执政诸公怎么样？"孔子道："咳！这班器识狭小的人算得什么？"

21. 子曰："不得中行而与之，必也狂狷乎！狂者进取，狷者有所不为也。"

孔子说："得不到言行合乎中庸的人和他相交，那一定要交到激进的人和狷介的人罢！激进者一意向前，狷介者也不肯做坏事。"

22. 子曰："南人有言曰：'人而无恒，不可以作巫医。'善夫！""不恒其德，或承之羞。"子曰："不占而已矣。"

孔子说："南方人有句话说：'人假若没有恒心，连巫医都做不了。'这句话很好呀！"

《易经·恒卦》的爻辞说："三心二意，翻云覆雨，总有人招致羞耻。"孔子又说："这话的意思是叫无恒心的人不必去占卦罢了。"

23. 子曰："君子和而不同，小人同而不和。"

孔子说："君子用自己的正确意见来纠正别人的错误意见，

21. The Master said, "Failing to find moderate men for associates, one would, if there is no alternative, have to turn to the undisciplined and the over-scrupulous. The former are enterprising, while the latter will draw the line at certain kinds of action."[4]

4. This saying, together with the saying in V.22, is quoted in the Mencius, VII.B.37 and commented upon at length.

22. The Master said, "The southerners have a saying: A man devoid of constancy[5] will not make a shaman or a doctor. How well said! 'If one does not show constancy in one's virtue, one will, perhaps, suffer shame.' "[6] The Master went on to comment, "The import of the saying is simply that in such a case there is no point in consulting the oracle."

5. Cf. VII.26.

6. The text to the third line of hexagram 32 *heng* (constancy).

23. The Master said, "The gentleman agrees with others without being an echo. The small man echoes without being in agree-

使一切都做到恰到好处，却不肯盲从附和。小人只是盲从附和，却不肯表示自己的不同意见。”

24. 子贡问曰：“乡人皆好之，何如?”

子曰：“未可也。”

“乡人皆恶之，何如?”

子曰：“未可也；不如乡人之善者好之，其不善者恶之。”

子贡问道:“满乡村的人都喜欢他，这个人怎么样?”孔子道:“还不行。”

子贡便又道:“满乡村的人都厌恶他，这个人怎么样?”孔子道:“还不行。最好是满乡村的好人都喜欢他，满乡村的坏人都厌恶他。”

25. 子曰：“君子易事而难说也。说之不以道，不说也；及其使人也，器之。小人难事而易说也。说之虽不以道，说也；及其使人也，求备焉。”

孔子说:“在君子底下工作很容易，讨他的欢喜却难。不用正当的方式去讨他的欢喜，他不会欢喜的；等到他使用人的时候，却衡量各人的才德去分配任务。在小人底下工作很难，讨他的欢喜却容易。用不正当的方式去讨他的欢喜，他会欢喜的；等到他使用人的时候，便会百般挑剔，求全责备。”

ment."

24. Zi-gong asked, "'All in the village like him.' What do you think of that?"

The Master said, "That is not enough."

"'All in the village dislike him.' What do you think of that?"

The Master said, "That is not enough either. It would be better if 'those in his village who are good like him and those who are bad dislike him.'"

25. The Master said, "The gentleman is easy to serve but difficult to please. He will not be pleased unless you try to please him by following the Way, but when it comes to employing the services of others, he does so within the limits of their capacity. The small man is difficult to serve but easy to please. He will be pleased even though you try to please him by not following the Way, but when it comes to employing the services of others, he demands all-round perfection."

子路篇第十三

26. 子曰："君子泰而不骄，小人骄而不泰。"

孔子说："君子安详舒泰，却不骄傲凌人；小人骄傲凌人，却不安详舒泰。"

27. 子曰："刚、毅、木、讷近仁。"

孔子说："刚强、果决、朴质而言语不轻易出口，有这四种品德的人近于仁德。"

28. 子路问曰："何如斯可谓之士矣？"

子曰："切切偲偲，怡怡如也，可谓士矣。朋友切切偲偲，兄弟怡怡。"

子路问道："怎么样才可以叫做'士'了呢？"孔子道："互相批评，和睦共处，可以叫做'士'了。朋友之间，互相批评；兄弟之间，和睦共处。"

29. 子曰："善人教民七年，亦可以即戎矣。"

孔子说："善人教导人民达七年之久，也能够叫他们作战了。"

30. 子曰："以不教民战，是谓弃之。"

孔子道："用未经受过训练的人民去作战，这等于糟踏生命。"

26. The Master said, "The gentleman is at ease without being arrogant;[7] the small man is arrogant without being at ease."

7. Cf. XX.2.

27. The Master said, "Unbending strength, resoluteness, simplicity and slowness of speech[8] are close to benevolence."

8. Cf. VII.3.

28. Zi-lu asked, "What must a man be like before he deserves to be called a Gentleman?"

The Master said, "One who is, on the one hand, earnest and keen and, on the other, genial deserves to be called a Gentleman— earnest and keen amongst friends and genial amongst brothers."

29. The Master said, "After a good man has trained the common people for seven years, they should be ready to take up arms."

30. The Master said, "To send the common people to war untrained is to throw them away."

宪问篇第十四

1. 宪问耻。子曰："邦有道，谷；邦无道，谷，耻也。"

"克、伐、怨、欲不行焉，可以为仁矣？"

子曰："可以为难矣，仁则吾不知也。"

原宪问如何叫耻辱。孔子道："国家政治清明，做官领薪俸；国家政治黑暗，做官领薪俸，这就是耻辱。"

原宪又道："好胜、自夸、怨恨和贪心四种毛病都不曾表现过，这可以说是仁人了吗？"孔子道："可以说是难能可贵的了，若说是仁人，那我不能同意。"

2. 子曰："士而怀居，不足以为士矣。"

孔子说："读书人而留恋安逸，便不配做读书人了。"

3. 子曰："邦有道，危言危行；邦无道，危行言孙。"

孔子说："政治清明，言语正直，行为正直；政治黑暗，行为正直，言语谦顺。"

4. 子曰："有德者必有言，有言者不必有德。仁者必有勇，勇者不必有仁。"

孔子说："有道德的人一定有名言，但有名言的人不一定有道德。仁人一定勇敢，但勇敢的人不一定仁。"

BOOK 14

1. Xian asked about the shameful. The Master said, "It is shameful to make salary your sole object, irrespective of whether the Way prevails in the state or not."

"Standing firm against the temptation to press one's advantage, to brag about oneself, to harbour grudges or to be covetous may be called 'benevolent'?"

The Master said, "It may be called 'difficult', but I don't know about its being benevolent."

2. The Master said, "A Gentleman who is attached to a settled home is not worthy of being a Gentleman."

3. The Master said, "When the Way prevails in the state, speak and act with perilous high-mindedness; when the Way does not prevail, act with perilous high-mindedness but speak with self-effacing diffidence."

4. The Master said, "A man of virtue is sure to be the author of memorable sayings, but the author of memorable sayings is not necessarily virtuous. A benevolent man is sure to possess courage, but a courageous man does not necessarily possess

宪问篇第十四

5. 南宫适问于孔子曰："羿善射，奡荡舟，俱不得其死然。禹稷躬稼而有天下。"夫子不答。

南宫适出，子曰："君子哉若人！尚德哉若人！"

南宫适向孔子问道："羿擅长射箭，奡擅长水战，都没有得到好死。禹和稷自己下地种田，却得到了天下。［怎样解释这些历史？］"孔子没有答复。

南宫适退了出来。孔子道："这个人，好一个君子！这个人，多么尊尚道德！"

6. 子曰："君子而不仁者有矣夫，未有小人而仁者也。"

孔子说："君子之中不仁的人有的罢，小人之中却不会有仁人。"

7. 子曰："爱之，能勿劳乎？忠焉，能勿诲乎？"

孔子说："爱他，能不叫他劳苦吗？忠于他，能够不教诲他吗？"

8. 子曰："为命，裨谌草创之，世叔讨论之，行人子羽修饰之，

benevolence."

5. Nan-gong Kuo asked Confucius, "Both Yi who was good at archery and Ao who could push a boat over dry land met violent deaths, while Yu and Ji who took part in planting the crops gained the Empire." The Master made no reply.

After Nan-gong Kuo had left, the Master commented, "How gentlemanly that man is! How reverent towards virtue he is!"

6. The Master said, "We may take it that there are cases of gentlemen who are unbenevolent, but there is no such thing as a small man who is benevolent."

7. The Master said, "Can you love anyone without making him work hard? Can you do your best for anyone without educating him?"

8. The Master said, "In the composition of the text of a treaty, Pi

东里子产润色之。”

孔子说：“郑国外交辞令的创制，裨谌拟稿，世叔提意见，外交官子羽修改，子产作文词上的加工。”

9. 或问子产。子曰：“惠人也。”

问子西。曰：“彼哉！彼哉！”

问管仲。曰：“人也。夺伯氏骈邑三百，饭疏食，没齿无怨言。”

有人向孔子问子产是怎样的人物。孔子道：“是宽厚慈惠的人。”

又问到子西。孔子道：“他呀，他呀！”

又问到管仲。孔子道：“他是人才。剥夺了伯氏骈邑三百户的采地，使伯氏只能吃粗粮，到死没有怨恨的话。”

10. 子曰：“贫而无怨难，富而无骄易。”

孔子说：“贫穷却没有怨恨，很难；富贵却不骄傲，倒容易做到。”

11. 子曰：“孟公绰为赵魏老则优，不可以为滕、薛大夫。”

Chen would write the draft, Shi Shu would make comments, Zi-yu, the master of protocol, would touch it up and Zi-chan of Dong Li would make embellishments."

9. Someone asked about Zi-chan. The Master said, "He was a generous man." He asked about Zi-xi. The Master said, "That man! That man!" He then asked about Guan Zhong. The Master said, "*He was a man.*[1] He took three hundred households from the fief of the Bo family in the city of Pian, and Bo, reduced to living on coarse rice, did not utter a single word of complaint to the end of his days."

1. The text is probably corrupt. In the light of the first answer, an adjective, probably "benevolent", should precede the word "man". See chapters 16 and 17 below where Guan Zhong is said to be "benevolent".

10. The Master said, "It is more difficult not to complain of injustice when poor than not to behave with arrogance when rich."

11. The Master said, "Meng Gong-chuo would be more than adequate as steward to great noble families like Zhao or Wei, but

孔子说："孟公绰，若是叫他做晋国诸卿赵氏、魏氏的家臣，那是力有余裕的；却没有才能来做滕、薛这样小国的大夫。"

12. 子路问成人。

子曰："若臧武仲之知，公绰之不欲，卞庄子之勇，冉求之艺，文之以礼乐，亦可以为成人矣。"曰："今之成人者何必然？见利思义，见危授命，久要不忘平生之言，亦可以为成人矣。"

子路问怎样才是全人。孔子道："智慧像臧武仲，清心寡欲像孟公绰，勇敢像卞庄子，多才多艺像冉求，再用礼乐来成就他的文采，也可以说是全人了。"等了一会，又道："现在的全人哪里一定要这样？看见利益便能想起该得不该得，遇到危险便肯付出生命，经过长久的穷困日子都不忘记平日的诺言，也可以说是全人了。"

13. 子问公叔文子于公明贾曰："信乎，夫子不言，不笑，不取乎？"

公明贾对曰："以告者过也。夫子时然后言，人不厌其言；乐然后笑，人不厌其笑；义然后取，人不厌其取。"

子曰："其然？岂其然乎？"

he would not be suitable as Counsellor even in a small state like Teng or Xue."

12. Zi-lu asked about the complete man.

The Master said, "A man as wise as Zang Wu-zhong, as free from desires as Meng Gong-chuo, as courageous as Zhuang-zi of Bian and as accomplished as Ran Qiu, who is further refined by the rites and music, may be considered a complete man." Then he added, "But to be a complete man nowadays one need not be all these things. If a man remembers what is right at the sight of profit, is ready to lay down his life in the face of danger, and does not forget sentiments he has repeated all his life even after having been long in straitened circumstances, he may be said to be a complete man."

13. The Master asked Gong-ming Jia about Kung-shu Wen-zi, "Is it true that your Master never spoke, never laughed and never took anything?"

Gong-ming Jia answered, "Whoever told you that exaggerated. My Master spoke only when it was time for him to speak. So people never grew tired of his speaking. He laughed

孔子向公明贾问到公叔文子，说："他老人家不言语，不笑，不取，是真的吗？"

公明贾答道："这是传话的人说错了。他老人家到应说话的时候才说话，别人不厌恶他的话；高兴了才笑，别人不厌恶他的笑；应该取才取，别人不厌恶他的取。"

孔子道："如此的吗？难道真是如此的吗？"

14. **子曰："臧武仲以防求为后于鲁，虽曰不要君，吾不信也。"**

孔子说："臧武仲［逃到齐国之前，］凭借着他的采邑防城请求立其子弟嗣为鲁国卿大夫，纵然有人说他不是要挟，我是不相信的。"

15. **子曰："晋文公谲而不正，齐桓公正而不谲。"**

孔子说："晋文公诡诈好耍手段，作风不正派；齐桓公作风正派，不用诡诈，不耍手段。"

16. **子路曰："桓公杀公子纠，召忽死之，管仲不死。"曰："未仁乎？"子曰："桓公九合诸侯，不以兵车，管仲之力也。如其仁，如其仁。"**

子路道："齐桓公杀了他哥哥公子纠，［公子纠的师傅］召忽因此自杀，［但是他的另一师傅］管仲却活着。"接着又

only when he was feeling happy. So people never grew tired of his laughing. He took only when it was right for him to take. So people never grew tired of his taking."

The Master said, "Can that really be the right explanation for the way he was, I wonder?"

14. The Master said, "Zang Wu-zhong used his fief to bargain for a successor to his line. Should it be said that he was not exerting pressure on his lord, I would not believe it."

15. The Master said, "Duke Wen of Jin was crafty and lacked integrity. Duke Huan of Qi, on the other hand, had integrity and was not crafty."

16. Zi-lu said, "When Duke Huan had Prince Jiu killed, Shao Hu died for the Prince but Guan Zhong failed to do so." He added, "In that case, did he fall short of benevolence?" The Master said, "It was due to Guan Zhong that Duke Huan was able, without a show of force, to assemble the feudal lords nine

道:“管仲该不是有仁德的吧?”孔子道:“齐桓公多次地主持诸侯间的盟会,停止了战争,都是管仲的力量。这就是管仲的仁德,这就是管仲的仁德。”

17.子贡曰:“管仲非仁者与?桓公杀公子纠,不能死,又相之。”

子曰:“管仲相桓公,霸诸侯,一匡天下,民到于今受其赐。微管仲,吾其被发左衽矣。岂若匹夫匹妇之为谅也,自经于沟渎而莫之知也?”

子贡道:“管仲不是仁人罢?桓公杀掉了公子纠,他不但不以身殉难,还去辅相他。”孔子道:“管仲辅相桓公,称霸诸侯,使天下一切得到匡正,人民到今天还受到他的好处。假若没有管仲,我们都会披散着头发,衣襟向左边开,[沦为落后民族]了。他难道要像普通老百姓一样守着小节小信,在山沟中自杀,还没有人知道的吗?”

18.公叔文子之臣大夫僎与文子同升诸公。子闻之,曰:“可以为‘文’矣。”

公叔文子的家臣大夫僎,[由于文子的推荐,]和文子一道做了国家的大臣。孔子知道这事,便道:“这便可以谥为

times. Such was his benevolence. Such was his benevolence."

17. Zi-gong said, "I don't suppose Guan Zhong was a benevolent man. Not only did he not die for Prince Jiu, but he lived to help Huan who had the Prince killed."

The Master said, "Guan Zhong helped Duke Huan to become the leader of the feudal lords and to save the Empire from collapse. To this day, the common people still enjoy the benefit of his acts. Had it not been for Guan Zhong, we might well be wearing our hair down and folding our robes to the left.[2] Surely his was not the petty faithfulness of the common man or woman who commits suicide in a ditch without anyone taking any notice."

2. i.e., in the fashion of the barbarians.

18. Counsellor Zhuan who had been an official in the household of Gong-shu Wen-zi was promoted to high office in the state, serving side by side with Gong-shu Wen-zi. On hearing of this, the Master commented, "Gong-shu Wen-zi deserved to be

‘文’了。”

19. 子言卫灵公之无道也，康子曰：“夫如是，奚而不丧?”

孔子曰：“仲叔圉治宾客，祝鮀治宗庙，王孙贾治军旅。夫如是，奚其丧?”

孔子讲到卫灵公的昏乱，康子道：“既然这样，为什么不败亡?”孔子道：“他有仲叔圉接待宾客，祝鮀管理祭祀，王孙贾统率军队，像这样，怎么会败亡?”

20. 子曰：“其言之不怍，则为之也难。”

孔子说：“那个人大言不惭，他实行就不容易。”

21. 陈成子弑简公。孔子沐浴而朝，告于哀公曰：“陈恒弑其君，请讨之。”公曰：“告夫三子!”

孔子曰：“以吾从大夫之后，不敢不告也。君曰‘告夫三

accorded the epithet '*wen*'."[3]

3. An account of the conferment of the posthumous title "*wen*" on Gong-shu Wen-zi is to be found in the Tan Gong 檀弓 chapter of the *Li Ji* 禮記. In the *Yi Zhou shu* 逸周书, it is said, among other things, that "bestowing rank on the common people is called '*wen*'". Cf. note to V.15.

19. When the Master spoke of the total lack of moral principle on the part of Duke Ling of Wei, Kang Zi commented, "That being the case, how is it he did not lose his state?"

Confucius said, "Zhong-shu Yu was responsible for foreign visitors, Priest Tuo for the ancestral temple and Wang-sun Jia for military affairs. That being the case, why should he have lost his state?"

20. The Master said, "Claims made immodestly are difficult to live up to."

21. Chen Cheng Zi killed Duke Jian. After washing himself ceremonially, Confucius went to court and reported to Duke Ai, saying, "Chen Heng has killed his lord. May I request that an

子’者!”

之三子告，不可。孔子曰：“以吾从大夫之后，不敢不告也。”

陈恒杀了齐简公。孔子斋戒沐浴而后朝见鲁哀公，报告道：“陈恒杀了他的君主，请你出兵讨伐他。”哀公道：“你向季孙、仲孙、孟孙三人去报告罢!”

孔子［退了出来,］道：“因为我曾忝为大夫，不敢不来报告，但是君上却对我说，‘给那三人报告吧’!”

孔子又去报告三位大臣，不肯出兵。孔子道：“因为我曾忝为大夫，不敢不报告。”

22.子路问事君。子曰：“勿欺也，而犯之。”

子路问怎样服侍人君。孔子道：“*不要［阳奉阴违地］欺骗他，却可以［当面］触犯他。*”

23.子曰：“君子上达，小人下达。”

孔子说：“*君子通达于仁义，小人通达于财利。*”

24.子曰：“古之学者为己，今之学者为人。”

army be sent to punish him?"

The Duke answered, "Tell the three noble lords."[4]

Confucius said, "I have reported this to you simply because I have a duty to do so, seeing that I take my place after the Counsellors, and now you say 'Tell the three noble lords.'"

He went and reported to the three noble lords, and they refused his request. Confucius said, "I have reported this to you simply because I have a duty to do so, seeing that I take my place after the Counsellors."[5]

4. i.e., the heads of the three powerful families in Lu.

5. The incident is recorded in the *Zuo zhuan* .

22. Zi-lu asked about the way to serve a lord. The Master said, "*Do not stand up to him while, all the time, you have been dishonest with him.*"

23. The Master said, "*The gentleman gets through to what is up above; the small man gets through to what is down below.*"[6]

6. Cf. chapter 35 below.

24. The Master said, "Men of antiquity studied to improve them-

孔子说：“古代学者的目的在修养自己的学问道德，现代学者的目的却在装饰自己，给别人看。”

25. 蘧伯玉使人于孔子。孔子与之坐而问焉，曰：“夫子何为？”对曰：“夫子欲寡其过而未能也。”

使者出。子曰：“使乎！使乎！”

蘧伯玉派一位使者访问孔子。孔子给他座位，而后问道：“他老人家干些什么？”使者答道：“他老人家想减少过错却还没能做到。”

使者辞了出来。孔子道：“好一位使者！好一位使者！”

26. 子曰：“不在其位，不谋其政。”

曾子曰：“君子思不出其位。”

曾子说：“君子所思虑的不超出自己的工作岗位。”

27. 子曰：“君子耻其言而过其行。”

孔子说：“说得多，做得少，君子以为耻。”

selves; men today study to impress others."

25. Qu Bo-yu sent a messenger to Confucius. Confucius sat with him and asked him, "What does your master do?" He answered, "My master seeks to reduce his errors but has not been able to do so."

When the messenger had left, the Master commented, "What a messenger! What a messenger!"

26. The Master said, "Do not concern yourself with matters of government unless they are the responsibility of the office you are in."[7]

Zeng Zi commented, "The gentleman does not allow his thoughts to go beyond his office."

7. This saying is also found in VIII. 14.

27. The Master said, "The gentleman is ashamed when the words he utters outstrip his deeds."

宪问篇第十四

28. 子曰："君子道者三，我无能焉：仁者不忧，知者不惑，勇者不惧。"

子贡曰："夫子自道也。"

孔子说："君子所行的三件事，我一件也没能做到：仁德的人不忧愁，智慧的人不迷惑，勇敢的人不惧怕。"子贡道："这正是他老人家对自己的叙述哩。"

29. 子贡方人。子曰："赐也贤乎哉？夫我则不暇。"

子贡讥评别人。孔子对他道："你就够好了吗？我却没有这闲工夫。"

30. 子曰："不患人之不己知，患其不能也。"

孔子说："不着急别人不知道我，只着急自己没有能力。"

31. 子曰："不逆诈，不亿不信，抑亦先觉者，是贤乎！"

孔子说："不预先怀疑别人的欺诈，也不无根据地猜测别

28. The Master said, "There are three things constantly on the lips of the gentleman none of which I have succeeded in following: 'A man of benevolence never worries;[8] a man of wisdom is never in two minds;[9] a man of courage is never afraid.'"[10]

Zi-gong said, "What the Master has just quoted is a description of himself."

8. about the future.

9. about right and wrong.

10. Cf. IX.29.

29. Zi-gong was given to grading people. The Master said, "How superior Ci is! For my part I have no time for such things."

30. The Master said, "It is not the failure of others to appreciate your abilities that should trouble you,[11] but rather your own lack of them."

11. This sentence is to be found in I.16. Cf. also I.1 and XV.19.

31. The Master said, "Is a man not superior who, without anticipating attempts at deception or presuming acts of bad faith, is,

人的不老实，却能及早发觉，这样的人是一位贤者罢！”

32. 微生亩谓孔子曰：“丘何为是栖栖者与？无乃为佞乎？”孔子曰：“非敢为佞也，疾固也。”

微生亩对孔子道：“你为什么这样忙忙碌碌的呢？不是要逞你的口才吗？”孔子道：“我不是敢逞口才，而是讨厌那种顽固不通的人。”

33. 子曰：“骥不称其力，称其德也。”

孔子说：“称千里马叫做骥，并不是赞美它的气力，而是赞美它的品质。”

34. 或曰：“以德报怨，何如？”子曰：“何以报德？以直报怨，以德报德。”

有人对孔子道：“拿恩惠来回答怨恨，怎么样？”孔子道：“拿什么来酬答恩惠呢？拿公平正直来回答怨恨，拿恩惠来酬答恩惠。”

nevertheless, the first to be alerted to such behaviour?"

32. Wei-sheng Mu said to Confucius, "Qiu, why are you so restless? Are you, perhaps, trying to practise flattery?"

Confucius answered, "I am not so impertinent as to practise flattery. It is just that I so detest inflexibility."

33. The Master said, "A good horse is praised for its virtue, not for its strength."

34. Someone said,

"Repay an injury with a good turn.[12]

What do you think of this saying?"

The Master said, "What, then, do you repay a good turn with? 'Repay an injury with straightness, but repay a good turn with a good turn.'"

12. Cf. "Do good to him who has done you an injury." (*Dao de jing*, chapter 63, p. 93)

宪问篇第十四

35. 子曰："莫我知也夫！"

子贡曰："何为其莫知子也？"

子曰："不怨天，不尤人，下学而上达。知我者其天乎！"

孔子叹道："没有人知道我呀！"子贡道："为什么没有人知道您呢？"孔子道："不怨恨天，不责备人，学习一些平常的知识，却透彻了解很高的道理。知道我的，只是天罢！"

36. 公伯寮愬子路于季孙。子服景伯以告，曰："夫子固有惑志于公伯寮，吾力犹能肆诸市朝。"

子曰："道之将行也与，命也；道之将废也与，命也。公伯寮其如命何！"

公伯寮向季孙毁谤子路。子服景伯告诉孔子，并且说："他老人家已经被公伯寮所迷惑了，可是我的力量还能把他的尸首在街头示众。"

孔子道："我的主张将实现吗，听之于命运；我的主张将永不实现吗，也听之于命运。公伯寮能把我的命运怎样呢！"

37. 子曰："贤者辟世，其次辟地，其次辟色，其次辟言。"

子曰："作者七人矣。"

孔子说："有些贤者逃避恶浊社会而隐居，次一等的择地

35. The Master said, "There is no one who understands me."

Zi-gong said, "How is it that there is no one who understands you?"

The Master said, "I do not complain against Heaven, nor do I blame Man. In my studies, I start from below and get through to what is up above. If I am understood at all, it is, perhaps, by Heaven."

36. Gong-bo Liao spoke ill of Zi-lu to Ji-sun. Zi-fu Jing-bo reported this, saying, "My master shows definite signs of being swayed by Gong-bo Liao, but I still have enough influence to have his carcass exposed in the market place."

The Master said, "It is Destiny if the Way prevails; it is equally Destiny if the Way falls into disuse. What can Gong-bo Liao do in defiance of Destiny?"

37. The Master said, "Men who shun the world come first; those who shun a particular place come next; those who shun a hostile look come next; those who shun hostile words come last."

而处，再次一等的避免不好的脸色，再次一等的回避恶言。”

孔子又说：“像这样的人已经有七位了。”

38.子路宿于石门。晨门曰：“奚自?”

子路曰：“自孔氏。”

曰：“是知其不可而为之者与?”

子路在石门住了一宵，［第二天清早进城,］司门者道：“从哪儿来?”子路道：“从孔家来。”司门者道：“就是那位知道做不到却定要去做的人吗?”

39.子击磬于卫，有荷蒉而过孔氏之门者，曰：“有心哉，击磬乎!”

既而曰：“鄙哉，硁硁乎！莫己知也，斯己而已矣。深则厉，浅则揭。”

子曰：“果哉！末之难矣。”

孔子在卫国，一天正敲着磬，有一个挑着草筐子的汉子恰在门前走过，便说道：“这个敲磬是有深意的呀!”等一会又说道：“磬声硁硁的，可鄙呀！［它好像在说，没有人知道我呀!］没有人知道自己，这就罢休好了。水深，索性连衣裳走过去；水浅，无妨撩起衣裳走过去。”

孔子道：“好坚决！没有办法说服他了。”

The Master said, "There were seven who got up."

38. Zi-lu put up for the night at the Stone Gate. The gatekeeper said, "Where have you come from?"

Zi-lu said, "From the Kongs'."

"Is that the Kong who keeps working towards a goal the realization of which he knows to be hopeless?"

39. While the Master was playing the stone chimes in Wei, a man who passed in front of the door, carrying a basket, said, "The way he plays the stone chimes is fraught with frustrated purpose." Presently he added, "How squalid this stubborn sound is. If no one understands him, [13] then he should give up, that is all.

When the water is deep, go across by wading;
When it is shallow, lift your hem and cross."[14]

The Master said, "That would be resolute indeed. Against such resoluteness there can be no argument."

13. Cf. chapter 35 above.

宪问篇第十四

40. 子张曰："《书》云：'高宗谅阴，三年不言。'何谓也？"

子曰："何必高宗，古之人皆然。君薨，百官总己以听于冢宰三年。"

子张道："《尚书》说：'殷高宗守孝，住在凶庐，三年不言语。'这是什么意思？"孔子道："不仅仅高宗，古人都是这样：国君死了，继承的君王三年不问政治，各部门的官员听命于宰相。"

41. 子曰："上好礼，则民易使也。"

孔子说："在上位的人若遇事依礼而行，就容易使百姓听从指挥。"

42. 子路问君子。子曰："修己以敬。"

曰："如斯而已乎？"曰："修己以安人。"

曰："如斯而已乎？"曰："修己以安百姓。修己以安百姓，尧舜其犹病诸？"

14. Ode 54.

40. Zi-zhang said, "The *Book of History* says,

Gao Zong confined himself to his mourning hut, and for three years remained silent.

What does this mean?"

The Master said, "There is no need to go to Gao Zong for an example. This was always so amongst men of antiquity. When the ruler died, all the officials joined together and placed themselves under the prime minister and, for three years, accepted his command."

41. The Master said, "When those above are given to the observance of the rites, the common people will be easy to command."[15]

15. Cf. XIII.4.

42. Zi-lu asked about the gentleman. The Master said, "He cultivates himself and thereby achieves reverence."

"Is that all?"

"He cultivates himself and thereby brings peace and securi-

宪问篇第十四

子路问怎样才能算是一个君子。孔子道："修养自己来严肃认真地对待工作。"

子路道："这样就够了吗？"孔子道："修养自己来使上层人物安乐。"

子路道："这样就够了吗？"孔子道："修养自己来使所有老百姓安乐。修养自己来使所有老百姓安乐，尧舜大概还没有完全做到哩！"

43. 原壤夷俟。子曰："幼而不孙弟，长而无述焉，老而不死，是为贼。"以杖叩其胫。

原壤两腿像八字一样张开坐在地上，等着孔子。孔子骂道："你幼小时候不懂礼节，长大了毫无贡献，老了还白吃粮食，真是个害人精。"说完，用拐杖敲了敲他的小腿。

44. 阙党童子将命。或问之曰："益者与？"子曰："吾见其居于位也，见其与先生并行也。非求益者也，欲速成者也。"

阙党的一个童子来向孔子传达信息。有人问孔子道："这小孩是肯求上进的人吗？"孔子道："我看见他［大模大样地］坐在位上，又看见他同长辈并肩而行。这不是个肯求上进的人，只是一个急于求成的人。"

ty to his fellow men."

"Is that all?"

"He cultivates himself and thereby brings peace and security to the people. Even Yao and Shun would have found the task of bringing peace and security to the people taxing."

43. Yuan Rang sat waiting with his legs spread wide. The Master said, "To be neither modest nor deferential when young, to have passed on nothing worthwhile when grown up, and to refuse to die when old, that is what I call a pest." So saying, the Master tapped him on the shin with his stick.

44. After a boy of Que Dang had announced a visitor, someone asked about him, saying, "Is he one who is likely to make progress?" The Master said, "I have seen him presume to take a seat and to walk abreast his seniors. He does not want to make progress. He is after quick results."

卫灵公篇第十五

1. 卫灵公问陈于孔子。孔子对曰："俎豆之事，则尝闻之矣；军旅之事，未之学也。"明日遂行。

卫灵公向孔子问军队陈列之法。孔子答道："礼仪的事情，我曾经听到过；军队的事情，从来没学习过。"第二天便离开卫国。

2. 在陈绝粮，从者病，莫能兴。子路愠见曰："君子亦有穷乎？"子曰："君子固穷，小人穷斯滥矣。"

孔子在陈国断绝了粮食，跟随的人都饿病了，爬不起床来。子路很不高兴地来见孔子，说道："君子也有穷得毫无办法的时候吗？"孔子道："君子虽然穷，还是坚持着；小人一穷便无所不为了。"

3. 子曰："赐也，女以予为多学而识之者与？"对曰："然，非与？"曰："非也，予一以贯之。"

孔子道："赐！你以为我是多多地学习又能够记得住的吗？"子贡答道："对呀，难道不是这样吗？"孔子道："不是的，我有一个基本观念来贯串它。"

BOOK 15

1. Duke Ling of Wei asked Confucius about military formations. Confucius answered, "I have, indeed, heard something about the use of sacrificial vessels, but I have never studied the matter of commanding troops." The next day he departed.

2. In Chen when provisions ran out the followers[1] had become so weak that none of them could get to their feet. Zi-lu, with resentment written all over his face, said, "Are there times when even gentlemen are brought to such extreme straits?" The Master said, "It comes as no surprise to the gentleman to find himself in extreme straits. The small man finding himself in extreme straits would throw over all restraint."

1. of Confucius.

3. The Master said, "Ci, do you think that I am the kind of man who learns widely and retains what he has learned in his mind?"

"Yes, I do. Is it not so?"

"No. I have a single thread binding it all together."[2]

2. Cf. IV.15.

卫灵公篇第十五

4. 子曰："由！知德者鲜矣。"

孔子对子路道："由！懂得'德'的人可少啦。"

5. 子曰："无为而治者其舜也与?夫何为哉?恭己正南面而已矣。"

孔子说："自己从容安静而使天下太平的人大概只有舜吧？他干了什么呢？庄严端正地坐朝廷罢了。"

6. 子张问行。子曰："言忠信，行笃敬，虽蛮貊之邦，行矣。言不忠信，行不笃敬，虽州里，行乎哉?立则见其参于前也，在舆则见其倚于衡也，夫然后行。"

子张书诸绅。

子张问如何才能使自己到处行得通。孔子道："言语忠诚老实，行为忠厚严肃，纵到了别的部族国家，也行得通。言语欺诈无信，行为刻薄轻浮，就是在本乡本土，能行得通吗？站立的时候，就［仿佛］看见'忠诚老实忠厚严肃'几个字在我们面前；在车厢里，也［仿佛］看见它刻在前面的横木上；［时时刻刻记着它，］这才能使自己到处行得通。"子张把这些话写在大带上。

BOOK 15

4. The Master said, "You, rare are those who understand virtue."

5. The Master said, "If there was a ruler who achieved order without taking any action, it was, perhaps, Shun. What was there to do but to hold himself in a respectful posture and to face due south?"[3]

3. The seat of the emperor faces south.

6. Zi-zhang asked about going forward without obstruction. The Master said, "If in word you are conscientious and trustworthy and in deed single-minded and reverent, then even in the lands of the barbarians you will go forward without obstruction. But if you fail to be conscientious and trustworthy in word or to be single-minded and reverent in deed, then can you be sure of going forward without obstruction even in your own neighbourhood? When you stand you should have this ideal there in front of you, and when you are in your carriage you should see it leaning against the handle-bar. Only then are you sure to go forward without obstruction."

Zi-zhang wrote this down on his sash.

7. 子曰：“直哉史鱼！邦有道，如矢；邦无道，如矢。君子哉蘧伯玉！邦有道，则仕；邦无道，则可卷而怀之。”

孔子说：“好一个刚直不屈的史鱼！政治清明也像箭一样直，政治黑暗也像箭一样直。好一个君子蘧伯玉！政治清明就出来做官，政治黑暗就可以把自己的本领收藏起来。”

8. 子曰：“可与言而不与之言，失人；不可与言而与之言，失言。知者不失人，亦不失言。”

孔子说：“可以同他谈，却不同他谈，这是错过人才；不可以同他谈，却同他谈，这是浪费言语。聪明人既不错过人才，也不浪费言语。”

9. 子曰：“志士仁人，无求生以害仁，有杀身以成仁。”

孔子说：“志士仁人，不贪生怕死因而损害仁德，只勇于牺牲来成全仁德。”

BOOK 15

7. The Master said, "How straight Shi Yu is! When the Way prevails in the state he is as straight as an arrow, yet when the Way falls into disuse in the state he is still as straight as an arrow.

"How gentlemanly Qu Bo-yu is! When the Way prevails in the state he takes office, but when the Way falls into disuse in the state he allows himself to be furled and put away."[4]

4. Cf. VII. 11.

8. The Master said, "To fail to speak to a man who is capable of benefiting is to let a man go to waste. To speak to a man who is incapable of benefiting is to let one's words go to waste. A wise man lets neither men nor words go to waste."

9. The Master said, "For Gentlemen of purpose and men of benevolence while it is inconceivable that they should seek to stay alive at the expense of benevolence, it may happen that they have to accept death in order to have benevolence accomplished."

卫灵公篇第十五

10. 子贡问为仁。子曰："工欲善其事，必先利其器。居是邦也，事其大夫之贤者，友其士之仁者。"

子贡问怎样去培养仁德。孔子道："工人要搞好他的工作，一定先要搞好他的工具。我们住在一个国家，就要敬奉那些大官中的贤人，结交那些士人中的仁人。"

11. 颜渊问为邦。子曰："行夏之时，乘殷之辂，服周之冕，乐则《韶》、《舞》。放郑声，远佞人。郑声淫，佞人殆。"

颜渊问怎样去治理国家。孔子道："用夏朝的历法，坐殷朝的车子，戴周朝的礼帽，音乐就用《韶》和《武》。舍弃郑国的乐曲，斥退小人。郑国的乐曲靡曼淫秽，小人危险。"

12. 子曰："人无远虑，必有近忧。"

孔子说："一个人没有长远的考虑，一定会有眼前的忧患。"

13. 子曰："已矣乎！吾未见好德如好色者也。"

孔子说："完了吧！我从没见过像喜欢美貌一般地喜欢美德

10. Zi-gong asked about the practice of benevolence. The Master said, "A craftsman who wishes to practise his craft well must first sharpen his tools. You should, therefore, seek the patronage of the most distinguished Counsellors and make friends with the most benevolent Gentlemen in the state where you happen to be residing."

11. Yan Yuan asked about the government of a state. The Master said, "Follow the calendar of the Xia, ride in the carriage of the Yin, and wear the ceremonial cap of the Zhou, but, for music, adopt the *shao* and the *wu*.[5] Banish the tunes of Zheng and keep plausible men at a distance. The tunes of Zheng are wanton and plausible men are dangerous."

5. For *shao* and *wu* see III.25.

12. The Master said, "A man who takes no thought for the distant future is sure to be beset by worries close at hand."

13. The Master said, "I suppose I should give up hope. I have yet to meet the man who is as fond of virtue as he is of beauty in

的人哩。”

14. 子曰：“臧文仲其窃位者与！知柳下惠之贤而不与立也。”

孔子说：“臧文仲大概是个做官不管事的人，他明知柳下惠贤良，却不给他官位。”

15. 子曰：“躬自厚而薄责于人，则远怨矣。”

孔子说：“重责备自己，而轻责备别人，怨恨自然不会来了。”

16. 子曰：“不曰‘如之何，如之何’者，吾末如之何也已矣。”

孔子说：“[一个人]不想想‘怎么办，怎么办’的，对这种人，我也不知道怎么办了。”

17. 子曰：“群居终日，言不及义，好行小慧，难矣哉！”

孔子说：“同大家整天在一块，不说一句有道理的话，只喜欢卖弄小聪明，这种人真难教导！”

women."

14. The Master said, "Is Zang Wen–Zhong not one who does not deserve his position? He knew the excellence of Liu Xia Hui and yet would not give him an appropriate position."[6]

6. This remark by Confucius, in a slightly different form, is also found in the *Zuo zhuan*.

15. The Master said, "If one sets strict standards for oneself and makes allowances for others when making demands on them, one will stay clear of ill will."

16. The Master said, "There is nothing I can do with a man who is not constantly saying, 'What am I to do? What am I to do?'"

17. The Master said, "Men spending all day together merely to indulge themselves in acts of petty cleverness without ever touching on the subject of morality in their conversation are sure to be in difficulty!"

18. 子曰："君子义以为质，礼以行之，孙以出之，信以成之。君子哉！"

孔子说："君子［对于事业］，以合宜为原则，依礼节实行它，用谦逊的言语说出它，用诚实的态度完成它。真是位君子呀！"

19. 子曰："君子病无能焉，不病人之不己知也。"

孔子说："君子只惭愧自己没有能力，不怨恨别人不知道自己。"

20. 子曰："君子疾没世而名不称焉。"

孔子说："到死而名声不被人家称述，君子引以为恨。"

21. 子曰："君子求诸己，小人求诸人。"

孔子说："君子要求自己，小人要求别人。

22. 子曰："君子矜而不争，群而不党。"

孔子说："君子庄矜而不争执，合群而不闹宗派。"

18. The Master said, "The gentleman has morality as his basic stuff and by observing the rites puts it into practice, by being modest gives it expression, and by being trustworthy in word brings it to completion. Such is a gentleman indeed!"

19. The Master said, "The gentleman is troubled by his own lack of ability, not by the failure of others to appreciate him."[7]

7. Cf. I.1, XIV.30.

20. The Master said, "The gentleman detests not leaving a name behind when he is gone."

21. The Master said, "What the gentleman seeks, he seeks within himself; what the small man seeks, he seeks in others."

22. The Master said, "The gentleman is conscious of his own superiority without being contentious, and comes together with other gentlemen without forming cliques."

23. 子曰："君子不以言举人，不以人废言。"

孔子说："君子不因为人家一句话［说得好］便提拔他，不因为他是坏人而鄙弃他的好话。"

24. 子贡问曰："有一言而可以终身行之者乎？"子曰："其恕乎！己所不欲，勿施于人。"

子贡问道："有没有一句可以终身奉行的话呢？"孔子道："大概是'恕'吧！自己所不想要的任何事物，就不要加给别人。"

25. 子曰："吾之于人也，谁毁谁誉？如有所誉者，其有所试矣。斯民也，三代之所以直道而行也。"

孔子说："我对于别人，诋毁了谁？称赞了谁？假若我有所称赞，必然是曾经考验过他的。夏、商、周三代的人都如此，所以三代能直道而行。"

26. 子曰："吾犹及史之阙文也。有马者借人乘之，今亡矣夫！"

23. The Master said, "The gentleman does not recommend a man on account of what he says, neither does he dismiss what is said on account of the speaker."

24. Zi-gong asked, "Is there a single word which can be a guide to conduct throughout one's life?"

The Master said, "It is perhaps the word 'shu'.[8] Do not impose on others what you yourself do not desire."

8. i.e., using oneself as a measure in gauging the wishes of others. Cf. IV. 15 and VI.30. It is interesting to note that in V. 12 when Zi-gong remarked that if he did not wish others to impose on him neither did he wish to impose on others, Confucius' comment was that this was beyond his ability.

25. The Master said, "Whom among men have I ever praised or condemned? If there is anyone I praised, you may be sure that he had been put to the test. These common people are the touchstone by which the Three Dynasties were kept to the straight path."

26. The Master said, "I am old enough to have seen scribes who

孔子说："我还能够看到史书存疑的地方。有马的人［自己不会训练，］先给别人使用，这种精神，今天也没有了吧!"

27. 子曰："巧言乱德。小不忍，则乱大谋。"

孔子说："花言巧语足以败坏道德。小事情不忍耐，便会败坏大事情。"

28. 子曰："众恶之，必察焉；众好之，必察焉。"

孔子说："大家厌恶他，一定要去考察；大家喜爱他，也一定要去考察。"

29. 子曰："人能弘道，非道弘人。"

孔子说："人能够把道廓大，不是用道来廓大人。"

30. 子曰："过而不改，是谓过矣。"

孔子说："有错误而不改正，那个错误便真叫做错误了。"

lacked refinement. Those who had horses would permit others to drive them.[9] Nowadays, there are, I suppose, no longer such cases."

9. One's carriages and horses are not things one should lightly permit others to use. To do so shows, therefore, a lack of refinement.

27. The Master said, "Artful words will ruin one's virtue; the lack of self–restraint in small matters will bring ruin to great plans."

28. The Master said, "Be sure to go carefully into the case of the man who is disliked by the multitude. Be sure to go carefully into the case of the man who is liked by the multitude."[10]

10. Cf. XIII. 24.

29. The Master said, "It is Man who is capable of broadening the Way. It is not the Way that is capable of broadening Man."

30. The Master said, "Not to mend one's ways when one has erred is to err indeed."

31. 子曰："吾尝终日不食，终夜不寝，以思，无益，不如学也。"

孔子说："我曾经整天不吃，整晚不睡，去想，没有益处，不如去学习。"

32. 子曰："君子谋道不谋食。耕也，馁在其中矣；学也，禄在其中矣。君子忧道不忧贫。"

孔子说："君子用心力于学术，不用心力于衣食。耕田，也常常饿着肚皮；学习，常常得到俸禄。君子只着急得不到道，不着急得不到财。"

33. 子曰："知及之，仁不能守之；虽得之，必失之。知及之，仁能守之。不庄以莅之，则民不敬。知及之，仁能守之，庄以莅之，动之不以礼，未善也。"

孔子说："聪明才智足以得到它，仁德不能保持它；就是得到，一定会丧失。聪明才智足以得到它，仁德能保持它。不用严肃态度来治理百姓，百姓也不会认真［地生活和工作］。聪明才智足以得到它，仁德能保持它，能用严肃的态度来治理百姓，假若不合理合法地动员百姓，是不够好的。"

BOOK 15

31. The Master said, "Once I went without food all day and without sleep all night thinking, but I found that this did me no good at all. It would have been better for me to have spent the time in learning."

32. The Master said, "The gentleman devotes his mind to attaining the Way and not to securing food. Go and till the land and you will end up by being hungry, as a matter of course; study, and you will end up with the salary of an official, as a matter of course. The gentleman worries about the Way, not about poverty."

33. The Master said, "What is within the reach of a man's understanding but beyond the power of his benevolence to keep is something he will lose even if he acquires it. A man may be wise enough to attain it and benevolent enough to keep it, but if he does not rule over them with dignity, then the common people will not be reverent. A man may be wise enough to attain it, benevolent enough to keep it and may govern the people with dignity, but if he does not set them to work in accordance with the rites, he still falls short of perfection."

卫灵公篇第十五

34. 子曰："君子不可小知而可大受也，小人不可大受而可小知也。"

孔子道："君子不可以用小事情考验他，却可以接受重大任务；小人不可以接受重大任务，却可以用小事情考验他。"

35. 子曰："民之于仁也，甚于水火。水火，吾见蹈而死者矣，未见蹈仁而死者也。"

孔子说："百姓需要仁德，更急于需要水火。往水火里去，我看见因而死了的，却从没有看见践履仁德因而死了的。"

36. 子曰："当仁，不让于师。"

孔子说："面临着仁德，就是老师，也不同他谦让。"

37. 子曰："君子贞而不谅。"

孔子说："君子讲大信，却不讲小信。"

38. 子曰："事君，敬其事而后其食。"

孔子说："对待君上，认真工作，把拿俸禄的事放在后面。"

BOOK 15

34. The Master said, "The gentleman cannot be valued on the strength of small matters but can be given great responsibilities. A small man cannot be given great responsibilities but can be valued on the strength of small matters."

35. The Master said, "*The common people exercise a more extreme caution towards benevolence than even towards water and fire.* In the case of water and fire, I have seen men die by stepping on them, but I have never seen any man die by stepping on benevolence."

36. The Master said, "When faced with the opportunity to practise benevolence do not yield precedence even to your teacher."

37. The Master said, "*The gentleman is steadfast in purpose but he is not inflexible.*"

38. The Master said, "In serving one's lord, one should approach one's duties with reverence and relegate reward to second place."

卫灵公篇第十五

39. 子曰：“有教无类。”

孔子说：“人人我都教育，没有［贫富、地域等等］区别。”

40. 子曰：“道不同，不相为谋。”

孔子说：“主张不同，不互相商议。”

41. 子曰：“辞达而已矣。”

孔子说：“言辞，足以达意便罢了。”

42. 师冕见，及阶，子曰：“阶也。”及席，子曰：“席也。”皆坐，子告之曰：“某在斯，某在斯。”

师冕出。子张问曰：“与师言之道与？”子曰：“然；固相师之道也。”

师冕来见孔子，走到阶沿，孔子道：“这是阶沿啦。”走到坐席旁，孔子道：“这是坐席啦。”都坐定了，孔子告诉他说：“某人在这里，某人在这里。”

师冕辞了出来。子张问道：“这是同瞎子讲话的方式吗？”孔子道：“对的；这本来是帮助瞎子的方式。”

BOOK 15

39. The Master said, *"In instruction there is no grading into categories."*

40. The Master said, "There is no point in people taking counsel together who follow different ways."

41. The Master said, "It is enough that the language one uses should get the point across."

42. Mian, the Master Musician, [11] called. When he came to the steps, the Master said, "You have reached the steps," and when he came to the mat, the Master said, "You have reached the mat." When everyone was seated, the Master told him, "This is So-and-so here and that is So-and-so over there."

After the Master Musician had gone, Zi-zhang asked, "Is that the way to talk to a musician?" The Master said, "Yes. That is the way to assist a musician."

11. In this period the musical profession was confined to the blind.

季氏篇第十六

1. 季氏将伐颛臾。冉有、季路见于孔子曰："季氏将有事于颛臾。"

孔子曰："求！无乃尔是过与？夫颛臾，昔者先王以为东蒙主，且在邦域之中矣，是社稷之臣也。何以伐为？"

冉有曰："夫子欲之，吾二臣者皆不欲也。"

孔子曰："求！周任有言曰：'陈力就列，不能者止。'危而不持，颠而不扶，则将焉用彼相矣？且尔言过矣，虎兕出于柙，龟玉毁于椟中，是谁之过与？"

冉有曰："今夫颛臾，固而近于费。今不取，后世必为子孙忧。"

孔子曰："求！君子疾夫舍曰欲之而必为之辞。丘也闻有国有家者，不患寡而患不均，不患贫而患不安。盖均无贫，和无寡，安无倾。夫如是，故远人不服，则修文德以来之。既来之，则安之。今由与求也，相夫子，远人不服，而不能来也；邦分崩离析，而不能守也；而谋动干戈于邦内。吾恐季孙之忧，不在颛臾，而在萧墙之内也。"

季氏准备攻打颛臾。冉有、子路两人谒见孔子，说道："季氏准备对颛臾使用兵力。"

孔子道："冉求！这难道不应该责备你吗？颛臾，上代的君王曾经授权他主持东蒙山的祭祀，而且它的国境早在我们最初被封时的疆土之中，这正是和鲁国共安危存亡的藩属，为

BOOK 16

1. The head of the Ji family was going to launch an attack on Zhuan Yu. Ran You and Zi-lu went to see Confucius and said, "The Ji family are going to take action against Zhuan Yu."

Confucius said, "Qiu, surely it is you who are at fault? Formerly, a royal ancestor of ours gave Zhuan Yu the responsibility of sacrificing to the Dong Meng Mountain; moreover, their territory now lies within our boundaries. Thus they are a bulwark of the state. What reason can there be for attacking them?"

Ran You said, "It is what our master wishes. Neither of us is in favour of it."

Confucius said, "Qiu, there is a saying of Zhou Ren's which goes: displaying your strength you join the ranks, but, finding yourself wanting, you give up. What use to a blind man is the assistant who does not steady him when he totters or support him when he falls. Moreover, what you said is quite wrong. Whose fault is it when the tiger and the rhinoceros escape from their cages or when the tortoise shell and the jade are destroyed in their caskets?"

Ran You said, "But Zhuan Yu is strongly fortified and close to Bi. If it is not taken now, it is sure to be a source of trouble

什么要去攻打它呢?"

冉有道:"季孙要这么干，我们两人本来都是不同意的。"

孔子道:"冉求! 周任有句话说:'能够贡献自己的力量，这再任职；如果不行，就该辞职。'譬如瞎子遇到危险，不去扶持；将要摔倒了，不去搀扶，那又何必用助手呢?你的话是错了。老虎犀牛从槛里逃了出来，龟壳美玉在匣子里毁坏了，这是谁的责任呢?"

冉有道:"颛臾，城墙既然坚牢，而且离季孙的采邑费地很近。现今不把它占领，日子久了，一定会给子孙留下祸害。"

孔子道:"冉求! 君子就讨厌 [那种态度,] 不说自己贪心无厌，却一定另找借口。我听说过:无论是诸侯或者大夫，不必着急财富不多，只需着急财富不均；不必着急人民太少，只需着急境内不安。若是财富平均，便无所谓贫穷；境内和平团结，便不会觉得人少；境内平安，便不会倾危。做到这样，远方的人还不归服，便再修仁义礼乐的政教来招致他们。他们来了，就得使他们安心。如今仲由和冉求两人辅相季孙，远方之人不归服，却不能招致；国家支离破碎，却不能保全；反而想在国境以内使用兵力。我恐怕季孙的忧愁不在颛臾，却在鲁君哩。"

for the descendants of our master in the future."

Confucius said, "Qiu, the gentleman detests those who, rather than saying outright that they want something, can be counted on to offer a plausible pretext instead. What I have heard is that the head of a state or a noble family worries not about underpopulation but about uneven distribution, not about poverty but about instability.[1] For where there is even distribution there is no such thing as poverty, where there is harmony there is no such thing as underpopulation and where there is stability there is no such thing as overturning. It is for this reason that when distant subjects are unsubmissive one cultivates one's moral quality in order to attract them, and once they have come one makes them content. But you and You have not been able either to help your master to attract the distant subjects when they are unsubmissive or to preserve the state when it is disintegrating. Instead, you propose to resort to the use of arms within the state itself. I am afraid that Ji-sun's worries lie not in Zhuan Yu but within the walls of his palace."

1. The text is corrupt here. In the light of what follows, the passage should, probably, read: "... worries not about poverty but about uneven distribution, not about underpopulation but about disharmony,

季氏篇第十六

2. 孔子曰："天下有道，则礼乐征伐自天子出；天下无道，则礼乐征伐自诸侯出。自诸侯出，盖十世希不失矣；自大夫出，五世希不失矣；陪臣执国命，三世希不失矣。天下有道，则政不在大夫。天下有道，则庶人不议。"

孔子说："天下太平，制礼作乐以及出兵都决定于天子；天下昏乱，制礼作乐以及出兵便决定于诸侯。决定于诸侯，大概传到十代，很少还能继续的；决定于大夫，传到五代，很少还能继续的；若是大夫的家臣把持国家政权，传到三代很少还能继续的。天下太平，国家的最高政治权力就不会掌握在大夫之手。天下太平，老百姓就不会议论纷纷。"

3. 孔子曰："禄之去公室五世矣，政逮于大夫四世矣，故夫三桓之子孙微矣。"

孔子说："国家政权离开了鲁君，[从鲁君来说，]已经五代了；政权到了大夫之手，[从季氏来说，]已经四代了，所

not about overturning but about instability."

2. Confucius said, "When the Way prevails in the Empire, the rites and music and punitive expeditions are initiated by the Emperor. When the Way does not prevail in the Empire, they are initiated by the feudal lords. When they are initiated by the feudal lords, it is surprising if power does not pass from their descendants within ten generations. When they are initiated by the Counsellors, it is surprising if power does not pass from their descendants within five generations. When the prerogative to command in a state is in the hands of officials of the Counsellors it is surprising if power does not pass from their descendants within three generations. When the Way prevails in the Empire, policy does not rest with the Counsellors. When the Way prevails in the Empire, the Commoners do not express critical views."

3. Confucius said, "It is five generation since patronage passed out of the control of the Ducal House. It is four generations since government came under the control of the Counsellors. For this reason the descendants of the three houses of Huan are on the

以桓公的三房子孙现在也衰微了。”

4. 孔子曰：“益者三友，损者三友。友直，友谅，友多闻，益矣。友便辟，友善柔，友便佞，损矣。”

孔子说：“有益的朋友三种，有害的朋友三种。同正直的人交友，同信实的人交友，同见闻广博的人交友，便有益了。同谄媚奉承的人交友，同当面恭维背面毁谤的人交友，同夸夸其谈的人交友，便有害了。”

5. 孔子曰：“益者三乐，损者三乐。乐节礼乐，乐道人之善，乐多贤友，益矣。乐骄乐，乐佚游，乐宴乐，损矣。”

孔子说：“有益的快乐三种，有害的快乐三种。以得到礼乐的调节为快乐，以宣扬别人的好处为快乐，以交了不少有益的朋友为快乐，便有益了。以骄傲为快乐，以游荡忘返为快乐，以饮食荒淫为快乐，便有害了。”

6. 孔子曰：“侍于君子有三愆：言未及之而言谓之躁，言及之而不言谓之隐，未见颜色而言谓之瞽。”

孔子说：“陪着君子说话容易犯三种过失:没轮到他说话，却先说，叫做急躁；该说话了，却不说，叫做隐瞒；不看看

decline."

4. Confucius said, "He stands to benefit who makes friends with three kinds of people. Equally, he stands to lose who makes friends with three other kinds of people. To make friends with the straight, the trustworthy in word and the well-informed is to benefit. To make friends with the ingratiating in action, the pleasant in appearance and the plausible in speech is to lose."

5. Confucius said, "He stands to benefit who takes pleasure in three kinds of things. Equally, he stands to lose who takes pleasure in three other kinds of things. To take pleasure in the correct regulation of the rites and music, in singing the praises of other men's goodness and in having a large number of excellent men as friends is to benefit. To take pleasure in showing off, in a dissolute life and in food and drink is to lose."

6. Confucius said, "When in attendance upon a gentleman one is liable to three errors. To speak before being spoken to by the gentleman is rash; not to speak when spoken to by him is to be evasive; to speak without observing the expression on his face

君子的脸色便贸然开口，叫做瞎眼睛。”

7. 孔子曰：“君子有三戒:少之时，血气未定，戒之在色；及其壮也，血气方刚，戒之在斗；及其老也，血气既衰，戒之在得。”

孔子说:“君子有三件事情应该警惕戒备:年轻的时候，血气未定，便要警戒，莫迷恋女色；等到壮大了，血气正旺盛，便要警戒，莫好胜喜斗；等到年老了，血气已经衰弱，便要警戒，莫贪求无厌。”

8. 孔子曰：“君子有三畏:畏天命，畏大人，畏圣人之言。小人不知天命而不畏也，狎大人，侮圣人之言。”

孔子说:“君子害怕的有三件事:怕天命，怕王公大人，怕圣人的言语。小人不懂得天命，因而不怕它；轻视王公大人，轻侮圣人的言语。”

9. 孔子曰：“生而知之者上也，学而知之者次也；困而学之，又其次也；困而不学，民斯为下矣。”

is to be blind."

7. Confucius said, "There are three things the gentleman should guard against. In youth when the blood and *qi*[2] are still unsettled he should guard against the attraction of feminine beauty. In the prime of life when the blood and *qi* have become unyielding, he should guard against bellicosity. In old age when the blood and *qi* have declined, he should guard against acquisitiveness."

2. *Qi* is the basic constituent of the universe. The refined *qi* fills the human body and, amongst other things, circulates with the blood.

8. Confucius said, "The gentleman stands in awe of three things. He is in awe of the Decree of Heaven. He is in awe of great men. He is in awe of the words of the sages. The small man, being ignorant of the Decree of Heaven, does not stand in awe of it. He treats great men with familiarity and the words of the sages with insolence."

9. Confucius said, "Those who are born with knowledge are the highest. Next come those who attain knowledge through study.

孔子说：“生来就知道的是上等，学习然后知道的是次一等；实践中遇见困难，再去学它，又是再次一等；遇见困难而不学，老百姓就是这种最下等的了。”

10. 孔子曰：“君子有九思：视思明，听思聪，色思温，貌思恭，言思忠，事思敬，疑思问，忿思难，见得思义。”

孔子说：“君子有九种考虑：看的时候，考虑看明白了没有；听的时候，考虑听清楚了没有；脸上的颜色，考虑温和么；容貌态度，考虑庄矜么；说的言语，考虑忠诚老实么；对待工作，考虑严肃认真么；遇到疑问，考虑怎样向人家请教；将发怒了，考虑有什么后患；看见可得的，考虑我是否应该得。”

11. 孔子曰：“见善如不及，见不善如探汤。吾见其人矣，吾闻其语矣。隐居以求其志，行义以达其道。吾闻其语矣，未见其人也。”

孔子说：“看见善良，努力追求，好像赶不上似的；遇见邪恶，使劲避开，好像将伸手到沸水里。我看见这样的人，也听过这样的话。避世隐居求保全他的意志，依义而行来贯彻他的主张。我听过这样的话，却没有见过这样的人。”

Next again come those who turn to study after having been vexed by difficulties. The common people, in so far as they make no effort to study even after having been vexed by difficulties, are the lowest."

10. Confucius said, "There are nine things the gentleman turns his thought to: to seeing clearly when he uses his eyes, to hearing acutely when he uses his ears, to looking cordial when it comes to his countenance, to appearing respectful when it comes to his demeanour, to being conscientious when he speaks, to being reverent when he performs his duties, to seeking advice when he is in doubt, to the consequences when he is enraged, and to what is right at the sight of gain."

11. Confucius said, "'Seeing what is good I act as if I risked failing to catch up with it; seeing what is not good I act as if I were testing hot water.' I have met such a man; I have heard such a claim.

"'I live in retirement in order to attain my purpose and practise what is right in order to realize my way.' I have heard such a claim, but I have yet to meet such a man."

12. 齐景公有马千驷，死之日，民无德而称焉。伯夷叔齐饿于首阳之下，民到于今称之。其斯之谓与？

齐景公有马四千匹，死了以后，谁都不觉得他有什么好行为可以称述。伯夷、叔齐两人饿死在首阳山下，大家到现在还称颂他们。那就是这个意思吧！

13. 陈亢问于伯鱼曰："子亦有异闻乎？"

对曰："未也。尝独立，鲤趋而过庭。曰：'学诗乎？'对曰：'未也。''不学诗，无以言。'鲤退而学诗。

他日，又独立，鲤趋而过庭。曰：'学礼乎？'对曰：'未也。''不学礼，无以立。'鲤退而学礼。闻斯二者。"

陈亢退而喜曰："问一得三，闻诗，闻礼，又闻君子之远其子也。"

陈亢向孔子的儿子伯鱼问道："您在老师那儿，也得着与众不同的传授吗？"

答道："没有。他曾经一个人站在庭中，我恭敬地走过。他问我道：'学诗没有？'我道：'没有。'他便道：'不学诗就不会说话。'我退回便学诗。过了几天，他又一个人站在庭中，

12. Duke Jing of Qi had a thousand teams of four horses each, but on his death the common people were unable to find anything for which to praise him, whereas Bo Yi and Shu Qi starved under Mount Shou Yang and yet to this day the common people still sing their praises. This is probably what is meant.[3]

3. This chapter is obviously defective. The beginning seems missing. Hence no speaker is mentioned. Neither is there any saying to which the final sentence can refer.

13. Chen Kang asked Bo-yu, "Have you not been taught anything out of the ordinary?"

"No, I have not. Once my father was standing by himself. As I crossed the courtyard with quickened steps,[4] he said, 'Have you studied the *Odes*?' I answered, 'No.' 'Unless you study the *Odes* you will be ill-equipped to speak.' I retired and studied the *Odes*.

"Another day, my father was again standing by himself. As I crossed the courtyard with quickened steps, he said, 'Have you studied the rites?' I answered, 'No.' 'Unless you study the rites you will be ill-equipped to take your stand.' I retired and studied the rites. I have been taught these two things."

我又恭敬地走过。他问道：'学礼没有？'我答：'没有。'他道：'不学礼，便没有立足社会的依据。'我退回便学礼。只听到这两件。"

陈亢回去非常高兴地道："我问一件事，知道了三件事。知道诗，知道礼，又知道君子对他儿子的态度。"

14. 邦君之妻，君称之曰夫人，夫人自称曰小童；邦人称之曰君夫人，称诸异邦曰寡小君；异邦人称之亦曰君夫人。

国君的妻子，国君称她为夫人，她自称为小童；国内的人称她为君夫人，但对外国人便称她为寡小君；外国人称她也为君夫人。

Chen Kang retired delighted and said, "I asked one question and got three answers. I learned about the *Odes*, I learned about the rites and I learned that a gentleman keeps his distance from his son."

4. as a sign of respect.

14. The lord of a state uses the term "lady" for his wife. She uses the term "little boy" for herself. The people of the state refer to her by the term "the lady of the lord", but when abroad they use the term "the little lord". People of other states also refer to her by the term "the lady of the lord."[5]

5. This is probably a ritual text which was copied into the blank space at the end of this scroll, and has nothing to do with the rest of the book.

阳货篇第十七

1. 阳货欲见孔子，孔子不见，归孔子豚。

孔子时其亡也，而往拜之。遇诸途。谓孔子曰："来！予与尔言。"曰："怀其宝而迷其邦，可谓仁乎？"曰："不可。——好从事而亟失时，可谓知乎？"曰："不可。——日月逝矣，岁不我与。"

孔子曰："诺；吾将仕矣。"

阳货想要孔子来拜会他，孔子不去，他便送孔子一个［蒸熟了的］小猪，［使孔子到他家来道谢］。

孔子探听他不在家的时候，去拜谢。

两人在路上碰着了。

他叫着孔子道："来！我同你说话。"［孔子走了过去。］他又道："自己有一身的本领，却听任着国家的事情糊里糊涂，可以叫做仁爱吗？"［孔子没吭声。］他便自己接口道："不可以。——一个人喜欢做官，却屡屡错过机会，可以叫做聪明吗？"［孔子仍然没吭声。］他又自己接口道："不可以。——时光一去，就不再回来了呀。"

孔子这才说道："好吧；我打算做官了。"

2. 子曰："性相近也，习相远也。"

孔子说："人性情本相近，因为习染不同，便相距悬远。"

BOOK 17

1. Yang Huo wanted to see Confucius, and when Confucius refused to go and see him he sent Confucius a present of a piglet.[1]

Confucius had someone keep watch on Yang Huo's house, and went to pay his respects during his absence. On the way he happened to meet Yang Huo who said to him, "Come now. I would speak with you." Then he went on, "Can the man be said to be benevolent who, while hoarding his treasure, allows the state to go astray? I should say not. Can the man be said to be wise who, while eager to take part in public life, constantly misses the opportunity? I should say not. The days and the months slip by. Time is not on our side."

Confucius said, "All right. I shall take office."

1. According to a version of this story in the Mencius, III.B.7, it was "a steamed piglet". (p. 127)

2. The Master said, "Men are close to one another by nature. They drift apart through behaviour that is constantly repeated."

阳货篇第十七

3. 子曰：“唯上知与下愚不移。”

孔子说：“只有上等的智者和下等的愚人是改变不了的。”

4. 子之武城，闻弦歌之声。夫子莞尔而笑，曰：“割鸡焉用牛刀?”

子游对曰：“昔者偃也闻诸夫子曰：‘君子学道则爱人，小人学道则易使也。’”

子曰：“二三子!偃之言是也。前言戏之耳。”

孔子到了［子游作县长］的武城，听到了弹琴瑟唱诗歌的声音。孔子微微笑着，说道：“宰鸡，何必用宰牛的刀？［治理这个小地方，用得着教育吗?］”

子游答道：“以前我听老师说过，做官的学习了，就会有仁爱之心；老百姓学习了，就容易听指挥，听使唤。［教育总是有用的。］”

孔子便向学生们道：“二三子！言偃的这话是正确的。我刚才那句话不过同他开玩笑罢了。”

5. 公山弗扰以费畔，召，子欲往。

子路不说，曰：“末之也，已，何必公山氏之之也?”

子曰：“夫召我者，而岂徒哉?如有用我者，吾其为东周乎?”

BOOK 17

3. The Master said, "It is only the most intelligent and the most stupid who cannot be budged."

4. The Master went to Wu Cheng. There he heard the sound of stringed instruments and singing. The Master broke into a smile and said, "Surely you don't need to use an ox-knife to kill a chicken."

Zi-you answered, "Some time ago I heard it from you, Master, that the gentleman instructed in the Way loves his fellow men and that the small man instructed in the Way is easy to command."

The Master said, "My friends, what Yan says is right. My remark a moment ago was only made in jest."

5. Gong-shan Fu-rao, using Bi as a stronghold, staged a revolt.[2] He summoned the Master and the Master wanted to go.

Zi-lu was displeased and said, "We may have nowhere to go, but why must we go to this person Gong-shan?"

公山弗扰盘踞在费邑图谋造反，叫孔子去，孔子准备去。

子路很不高兴，说道："没有地方去便算了，为什么一定要去公山氏那里呢？"

孔子道："那个叫我去的人，难道是白白召我吗？假若有人用我，我将使周文王、武王之道在东方复兴。"

6. 子张问仁于孔子。孔子曰："能行五者于天下为仁矣。"

"请问之。"

曰："恭，宽，信，敏，惠。恭则不侮，宽则得众，信则人任焉，敏则有功，惠则足以使人。"

子张向孔子问仁。孔子道："能够处处实行五种品德，便是仁人了。"

子张道："请问哪五种。"孔子道："庄重，宽厚，诚实，勤敏，慈惠。庄重就不致遭受侮辱，宽厚就会得到大众的拥护，诚实就会得到别人的任用，勤敏就会工作效率高、贡献大，慈惠就能够使唤人。"

7. 佛肸召，子欲往。

子路曰："昔者由也闻诸夫子曰：'亲于其身为不善者，君子不入也。'佛肸以中牟畔，子之往也，如之何？"

子曰："然，有是言也。不曰坚乎，磨而不磷；不曰白乎，

The Master said, "The man who summons me cannot be doing so for no purpose. If his purpose is to employ me, can I not, perhaps, create another Zhou in the east?"

2. against the Ji family, perhaps under the pretext of restoring power to the Duke of Lu.

6. Zi-zhang asked Confucius about benevolence. Confucius said, "There are five things and whoever is capable of putting them into practice in the Empire is certainly 'benevolent'."

"May I ask what they are?"

"They are respectfulness, tolerance, trustworthiness in word, quickness and generosity. If a man is respectful he will not be treated with insolence. If he is tolerant he will win the multitude. If he is trustworthy in word his fellow men will entrust him with responsibility. If he is quick he will achieve results. If he is generous his fellow men will be willing to do his bidding."

7. Bi Xi summoned the Master and the Master wanted to go.

Zi-lu said, "Some time ago I heard it from you, Master, that the gentleman does not enter the domain of one who in his

涅而不缁。吾岂匏瓜也哉?焉能系而不食?”

佛肸叫孔子，孔子打算去。

子路道:“从前我听老师说过:‘亲自做坏事的人那里，君子不去的。’如今佛肸盘踞中牟谋反，您却要去，怎么说得过去呢?”

孔子道:“对，我有过这话。但是，你不知道吗?最坚固的东西，磨也磨不薄；最白的东西，染也染不黑。我难道是匏瓜吗?哪里能够只是被悬挂着而不给人吃食呢?”

8. 子曰:“由也!女闻六言六蔽矣乎?”

对曰:“未也。”

“居!吾语女。好仁不好学，其蔽也愚；好知不好学，其蔽也荡；好信不好学，其蔽也贼；好直不好学，其蔽也绞；好勇不好学，其蔽也乱；好刚不好学，其蔽也狂。”

孔子说:“仲由!你听过有六种品德便会有六种弊病吗?”子路答道:“没有。”

孔子道:“坐下!我告诉你。爱仁德，却不爱学问，那种弊病就是容易被人愚弄；爱耍聪明，却不爱学问，那种弊病就是放荡而无基础；爱诚实，却不爱学问，那种弊病就是[容易被人利用，反而]害了自己；爱直率，却不爱学问，那种

own person does what is not good. Now Bi Xi is using Zhong Mou as a stronghold to stage a revolt. How can you justify going there?"

The Master said, "It is true, I did say that. But has it not been said, 'Hard indeed is that which can withstand grinding?' Has it not been said, 'White indeed is that which can withstand black dye?' Moreover, how can I allow myself to be treated like a gourd which, instead of being eaten, hangs from the end of a string?"

8. The Master said, "You, have you heard about the six qualities and the six attendant faults?"

"No."

"Be seated and I shall tell you. To love benevolence without loving learning is liable to lead to foolishness. To love cleverness without loving learning is liable to lead to straying from the right path. To love trustworthiness in word without loving learning is liable to lead to harmful behaviour. To love forthrightness without loving learning is liable to lead to being unrelenting. To love courage without loving learning is liable to lead to insubordination. To love unbending strength without

弊病就是说话尖刻，刺痛人心；爱勇敢，却不爱学问，那种弊病就是捣乱闯祸；爱刚强，却不爱学问，那种弊病就是胆大妄为。”

9. 子曰：“小子何莫学夫诗?诗，可以兴，可以观，可以群，可以怨。迩之事父，远之事君；多识于鸟兽草木之名。”

孔子说：“学生们为什么没有人研究诗?读诗，可以培养联想力，可以提高观察力，可以锻炼合群性，可以学得讽刺方法。近呢，可以运用其中道理来侍奉父母；远呢，可以用来服侍君上；而且多多认识鸟兽草木的名称。”

10. 子谓伯鱼曰：“女为《周南》、《召南》矣乎?人而不为《周南》、《召南》，其犹正墙面而立也与?”

孔子对伯鱼说道：“你研究过《周南》和《召南》了吗?人假若不研究《周南》和《召南》，那会像面正对着墙壁而站着罢!”

loving learning is liable to lead to indiscipline."[3]

3. Cf. Ⅷ.2.

9. The Master said, "Why is it none of you, my young friends, study the *Odes*? An apt quotation from the *Odes* may stimulate the imagination, *endow one with breeding*, enable one to live in a community and *give expression to grievances*.

"Inside the family there is the serving of one's father; outside, there is the serving of one's lord; there is also the acquiring of a wide knowledg

4. To these activities the study of the *Odes* must, presumably, be relevant, but the point is not explicitly made. This is very likely due to some corruption in the text.

10. The Master said to Bo-yu, "Have you studied the *Zhou nan* and *Shao nan*?[5] To be a man and not to study them is, I would say, to stand facing squarely the wall."[6]

5. These are the opening sections of the *Odes*.

6. Cf. XVI. 13.

11. 子曰："礼云礼云，玉帛云乎哉?乐云乐云，钟鼓云乎哉?"

孔子说："礼呀礼呀，仅是指玉帛等等礼物而说的吗?乐呀乐呀，仅是指钟鼓等等乐器而说的吗?"

12. 子曰："色厉而内荏，譬诸小人，其犹穿窬之盗也与?"

孔子说："颜色严厉，内心怯弱，若用坏人作比喻，怕像个挖洞跳墙的小偷罢!"

13. 子曰："乡愿，德之贼也。"

孔子说："没有真是非的好好先生是足以败坏道德的小人。"

14. 子曰："道听而途说，德之弃也。"

孔子说："听到道路传言就四处传播，这是应该革除的作风。"

15. 子曰："鄙夫可与事君也与哉?其未得之也，患不得之。既得之，患失之。苟患失之，无所不至矣。"

11. The Master said, "Surely when one says 'The rites, the rites,' it is not enough merely to mean presents of jade and silk. Surely when one says 'Music, music,' it is not enough merely to mean bells and drums."[7]

7. Cf. III.3.

12. The Master said, "A cowardly man who puts on a brave front is, when compared to small men, like the burglar who breaks in or climbs over walls."

13. The Master said, "The village worthy is the ruin of virtue."[8]

8. For Mencius' elaboration on this saying see the Mencius, VII.B.37.

14. The Master said, "The gossip-monger is the outcast of virtue."

15. The Master said, "Is it really possible to work side by side with a mean fellow in the service of a lord? Before he gets what he wants, he worries lest he should not get it. After he has got it,

孔子说:“鄙夫，难道能同他共事吗?当他没有得到职位的时候，生怕得不着；已经得着了，又怕失去。假若生怕失去，会无所不用其极了。”

16. 子曰:“古者民有三疾，今也或是之亡也。古之狂也肆，今之狂也荡；古之矜也廉，今之矜也忿戾；古之愚也直，今之愚也诈而已矣。”

孔子说:“古代的人民还有三种［可贵的］毛病，现在呢，或许都没有了。古代的狂人肆意直言，现在的狂人便放荡无羁了；古代自己矜持的人还有些不能触犯的地方，现在自己矜持的人却只是一味老羞成怒，无理取闹罢了；古代的愚人还直率，现在的愚人却只是欺诈要手段罢了。”

17. 子曰:“巧言令色，鲜矣仁。”

18. 子曰:“恶紫之夺朱也，恶郑声之乱雅乐也，恶利口之覆邦家者。”

孔子说:“紫色夺去了大红色的光彩和地位，可憎恶；郑国的乐曲破坏了典雅的乐曲，可憎恶；强嘴利舌颠覆国家，

he worries lest he should lose it, and when that happens he will stop at nothing."

16. The Master said, "In antiquity, the common people had three weaknesses, but today they cannot be counted on even to have these. In antiquity, in being wild, men were impatient of re-straint; today, in being wild, they simply deviate from the right path. In antiquity, in being conceited, men were uncompromis-ing; today, in being conceited, they are simply ill-tempered. In antiquity, in being foolish, men were straight; today, in being foolish, they are simply crafty."

17. The Master said, "It is rare, indeed, for a man with cunning words and an ingratiating countenance to be benevolent."[9]

9. This forms part of 1.3.

18. The Master said, "I detest purple for displacing vermillion. I detest the tunes of Zheng for corrupting classical music.[10] I de-test clever talkers who overturn states and noble families."

10. According to the traditional interpretation, vermillion is a pure colour

可憎恶。”

19. 子曰：“予欲无言。”子贡曰：“子如不言，则小子何述焉？”子曰：“天何言哉？四时行焉，百物生焉，天何言哉？”

孔子说：“我想不说话了。”子贡道：“您假若不说话，那我们传述什么呢？”孔子道：“天说了什么呢？四季照样运行，百物照样生长，天说了什么呢？”

20. 孺悲欲见孔子，孔子辞以疾。将命者出户，取瑟而歌，使之闻之。

孺悲来，要会晤孔子，孔子托言有病，拒绝接待。传命的人刚出房门，孔子便把瑟拿下来弹，并且唱着歌，故意使孺悲听到。

21. 宰我问：“三年之丧，期已久矣。君子三年不为礼，礼必坏；三年不为乐，乐必崩。旧谷既没，新谷既升，钻燧改火，期可已矣。”

子曰：“食夫稻，衣夫锦，于女安乎？”

while purple is a mixed colour, but by Confucius' time the practice of using purple in place of vermillion was becoming widespread. For Confucius' condemnation of the music of Zheng see V. 11.

19. The Master said, "I am thinking of giving up speech." Zi-gong said, "If you did not speak, what would there be for us, your juniors, to transmit?" The Master said, "What does Heaven ever say? Yet there are the four seasons going round and there are the hundred things coming into being. What does Heaven ever say?"

20. Ru Bei wanted to see Confucius. Confucius declined to see him on the grounds of illness. As soon as the man conveying the message had stepped out of the door, Confucius took his lute and sang, making sure that he heard it.

21. Zai Wo asked about the three-year mourning period, saying, "Even a full year is too long. If the gentleman gives up the practice of the rites for three years, the rites are sure to be in ruins; if he gives up the practice of music for three years, mu-

曰："安。"

"女安，则为之!夫君子之居丧，食旨不甘，闻乐不乐，居处不安，故不为也。今女安，则为之!"

宰我出。子曰："予之不仁也!子生三年，然后免于父母之怀。夫三年之丧，天下之通丧也，予也有三年之爱于其父母乎!"

宰我问道："父母死了，守孝三年，为期也太久了。君子有三年不去习礼仪，礼仪一定会废弃掉；三年不去奏音乐，音乐一定会失传。陈谷既已吃完了，新谷又已登场；打火用的燧木又经过了一个轮回，一年也就可以了。"

孔子道："[父母死了，不到三年，]你便吃那个白米饭，穿那个花缎衣，你心里安不安呢?"

宰我道："安。"

孔子便抢着道："你安，你就去干吧!君子的守孝，吃美味不晓得甜，听音乐不觉得快乐，住在家里不以为舒适，才不这样干。如今你既然觉得心安，便去干好了。"

宰我退了出来。孔子道："宰予真不仁呀!儿女生下地来，三年以后才能完全脱离父母的怀抱。替父母守孝三年，天下都是如此的。宰予难道就没有从他父母那里得着三年怀抱的爱护吗?"

sic is sure to collapse. A full year's mourning is quite enough. After all, in the course of a year, the old grain having been used up, the new grain ripens, and fire is renewed by fresh drilling."[11]

The Master said, "Would you, then, be able to enjoy eating your rice[12] and wearing your finery?"

"Yes. I would."

"If you are able to enjoy them, do so by all means. The gentleman in mourning finds no relish in good food, no pleasure in music, and no comforts in his own home. That is why he does not eat his rice and wear his finery. Since it appears that you enjoy them, then do so by all means."

After Zai Wo had left, the Master said, "How unfeeling Yu is. A child ceases to be nursed by his parents only when he is three years old. Three years' mourning is observed throughout the Empire. Was Yu not given three years' love by his parents?"

11. A different kind of wood is used for each of the four seasons so that the same wood is used again after a full year. This practice, presumably, had a ritual significance.

12. Rice was a luxury with millet being the staple food.

阳货篇第十七

22. 子曰："饱食终日，无所用心，难矣哉！不有博弈者乎？为之，犹贤乎已。"

孔子说："整天吃饱了饭，什么事也不做，不行的呀！不是有掷采下弈的游戏吗？干干也比闲着好。"

23. 子路曰："君子尚勇乎？"子曰："君子义以为上，君子有勇而无义为乱，小人有勇而无义为盗。"

子路问道："君子尊贵勇敢不？"孔子道："君子认为义是最可尊贵的，君子只有勇，没有义，就会捣乱造反；小人只有勇，没有义，就会做土匪强盗。"

24. 子贡曰："君子亦有恶乎？"子曰："有恶：恶称人之恶者，恶居下流而讪上者，恶勇而无礼者，恶果敢而窒者。"

曰："赐也亦有恶乎？""恶徼以为知者，恶不孙以为勇者，恶讦以为直者。"

子贡道："君子也有憎恨的事吗？"孔子道："有憎恨的事：憎恨一味传播别人的坏处的人，憎恨在下位而毁谤上级的人，

22. The Master said, "The man whose belly is full all day and who does not put his mind to some use is sure to meet with difficulties. Are there not such things as *bo* and *yi*?[13] Even playing these games is better than being idle."

13. While *yi* is the game known as *wei qi* 围棋 in later ages (better known in Western countries by its Japanese reading *go* 碁), *bo* is believed to have been a board game in which the moves of the pieces are decided by a throw of dice.

23. Zi-lu said, "Does the gentleman consider courage to be supreme?" The Master said, "For the gentleman it is morality that is considered supreme. Possessed of courage but devoid of morality, a gentleman will make trouble while a small man will be a brigand."

24. Zi-gong said, "Does even the gentleman have his dislikes?" The Master said, "Yes. The gentleman has his dislikes. He dislikes those who proclaim the evil in others. He dislikes those who, being in inferior positions, slander their superiors. He dislikes those who, while possessing courage, lack the spirit of the rites. He dislikes those whose resoluteness is not tempered by

憎恨勇敢却不懂礼节的人，憎恨勇于贯彻自己的主张，却顽固不通、执拗到底的人。”

孔子又道：“赐，你也有憎恶的事吗？”子贡随即答道：“我憎恨偷袭别人的成绩却作为自己的聪明的人，憎恨毫不谦虚却自以为勇敢的人，憎恨揭发别人阴私却自以为直率的人。”

25. 子曰：“唯女子与小人为难养也，近之则不孙，远之则怨。”

孔子道：“只有女子和小人是难得同他们共处的，亲近了，他会无礼；疏远了，他会怨恨。”

26. 子曰：“年四十而见恶焉，其终也已。”

孔子说：“到了四十岁还被厌恶，他这一生也就完了。”

understanding."

The Master added, "Do you, Ci, have your dislikes as well?"

"I dislike those in whom being unrelenting passes for wisdom. I dislike those in whom insolence passes for courage. I dislike those in whom exposure of others passes for forthrightness."

25. The Master said, "In one's household, it is the women and the small men that are difficult to deal with. If you let them get too close, they become insolent. If you keep them at a distance, they feel badly done by."

26. The Master said, "If by the age of forty a man is still disliked there is no hope for him."

微子篇第十八

1. 微子去之，箕子为之奴，比干谏而死。孔子曰：“殷有三仁焉。”

[纣王昏乱残暴,] 微子便离开了他，箕子做了他的奴隶，比干谏劝而被杀。孔子说：“殷商末年有三位仁人。”

2. 柳下惠为士师，三黜。人曰：“子未可以去乎？”曰：“直道而事人，焉往而不三黜？枉道而事人，何必去父母之邦？”

柳下惠做法官，多次地被撤职。有人对他说：“您不可以离开鲁国吗？”他道：“正直地工作，到哪里去不多次被撤职？不正直地工作，为什么一定要离开祖国呢？”

3. 齐景公待孔子曰：“若季氏，则吾不能；以季、孟之间待之。”曰：“吾老矣，不能用也。”孔子行。

齐景公讲到对待孔子的打算时说：“用鲁君对待季氏的模样对待孔子，那我做不到；我要用次于季氏而高于孟氏的待遇来对待他。”不久，又说道：“我老了，没有什么作为了。”孔子离开了齐国。

BOOK 18

1. The Viscount of Wei left him, the Viscount of Ji became a slave on account of him and Bi Gan lost his life for remonstrating with him.[1] Confucius commented, "There were three benevolent men in the Yin."

1. i.e., the tyrant Zhou.

2. Liu Xia Hui was dismissed three times when he was a judge. Someone said, "Is it not time for you to leave?"

"If, in the service of another, one is not prepared to bend the Way, where can one go without being dismissed three times? If, in the service of another, one is prepared to bend the Way, what need is there to leave the country of one's father and mother?"

3. In considering the treatment he should accord Confucius, Duke Jing of Qi said, "I am unable to accord him such exalted treatment as the Ji family receives."[2] So he placed him somewhere between the Ji and the Meng,[3] saying, "I am getting old. I am afraid I will not be able to put his talents to use." Confucius departed.

2. in Lu.

3. Both the Ji and the Meng were noble families in Lu.

微子篇第十八

4. 齐人归女乐，季桓子受之，三日不朝，孔子行。

齐国送了许多歌姬舞女给鲁国，季桓子接受了，三天不问政事，孔子就离职走了。

5. 楚狂接舆歌而过孔子曰："凤兮凤兮！何德之衰？往者不可谏，来者犹可追。已而，已而！今之从政者殆而！"

孔子下，欲与之言。趋而辟之，不得与之言。

楚国的狂人接舆一面走过孔子的车子，一面唱着歌，道："凤凰呀，凤凰呀！为什么这么倒霉？过去的不能再挽回，未来的还可不再着迷。算了吧，算了吧！现在的执政诸公危乎其危！"

孔子下车，想同他谈谈，他却赶快避开，孔子没法同他谈。

6. 长沮、桀溺耦而耕，孔子过之，使子路问津焉。

长沮曰："夫执舆者为谁？"

子路曰："为孔丘。"

曰："是鲁孔丘与？"

曰："是也。"

曰："是知津矣。"

BOOK 18

4. The men of Qi made a present of singing and dancing girls. Ji Huan Zi accepted them and stayed away from court for three days. Confucius departed.

5. Jie Yu, the Madman of Chu, went past Confucius, singing,

Phoenix, oh phoenix!
How thy virtue has declined!
What is past is beyond help,
What is to come is not yet lost.
Give up, give up!
Perilous is the lot of those in office today.

Confucius got down from his carriage with the intention of speaking with him but the Madman avoided him by hurrying off, and in the end Confucius was unable to speak with him.

6. Zhang Ju and Jie Ni were plougling together yoked as a team. Confucius went past them and sent Zi-lu to ask them where the ford was.

Zhang Ju said, "Who is that taking charge of the carriage?"[4]

Zi-lu said, "It is Kong Qiu."

"Then, he must be the Kong Qiu of Lu."

微子篇第十八

问于桀溺。

桀溺曰："子为谁?"

曰："为仲由。"

曰："是鲁孔丘之徒与?"

对曰："然。"

曰："滔滔者天下皆是也，而谁以易之?且而与其从辟人之士也，岂若从辟世之士哉?"耰而不辍。

子路行以告。

夫子怃然曰："鸟兽不可与同群，吾非斯人之徒与而谁与?天下有道，丘不与易也。"

长沮、桀溺两人一同耕田，孔子在那儿经过，叫子路去问渡口。

长沮问子路道："那位驾车子的是谁?"

子路道："是孔丘。"

他又道："是鲁国的那位孔丘吗?"

子路道："是的。"

他便道："他么，早晓得渡口在哪儿了。"

去问桀溺。

桀溺道："您是谁?"

子路道："我是仲由。"

桀溺道："您是鲁国孔丘的门徒吗?"

"He is."

"Then, he doesn't have to ask where the ford is."

Zi-lu asked Jie Ni.

Jie Ni said, "Who are you?"

"I am Zhong You."

"Then, you must be the disciple of Kong Qiu of Lu?"

Zi-lu answered, "I am."

"Throughout the Empire men are all the same. Who is there for you[5] to change places with? Moreover, for your own sake, would it not be better if, instead of following a Gentleman who keeps running away from men, [6] you followed one who runs away from the world altogether?"[7]

All the while he carried on harrowing without interruption.

Zi-lu went and reported what was said to Confucius.

The Master was lost in thought for a while and said, "One cannot associate with birds and beasts. Am I not a member of this human race? Who, then, is there for me to associate with? While the Way is to be found in the Empire, I will not change places with him."

4. The expression *zhi yu* is obscure and is likely to be corrupt.

5. Taking *er* as "you".

答道："对的。"

他便道："像洪水一样的坏东西到处都是，你们同谁去改革它呢？你与其跟着［孔丘那种］逃避坏人的人，为什么不跟着［我们这些］逃避整个社会的人呢？"说完，仍旧不停地做田里工夫。

子路回来报告给孔子。

孔子很失望地道："我们既然不可以同飞禽走兽合群共处，若不同人群打交道，又同什么去打交道呢？如果天下太平，我就不会同你们一道来从事改革了。"

7. 子路从而后，遇丈人，以杖荷蓧。

子路问曰："子见夫子乎？"

丈人曰："四体不勤，五谷不分。孰为夫子？"植其杖而芸。

子路拱而立。

止子路宿，杀鸡为黍而食之，见其二子焉。

明日，子路行以告。

子曰："隐者也。"使子路反见之。至，则行矣。

子路曰："不仕无义。长幼之节，不可废也；君臣之义，如之何其废之？欲洁其身，而乱大伦。君子之仕也，行其义也。道之不行，已知之矣。"

子路跟随着孔子，却远落在后面，碰到一个老头，用拐杖

BOOK 18

6. meaning Confucius.
7. meaning himself.

7. Zi–lu, when travelling with', fell behind. He met an old man, carrying a basket on a staff over his shoulder.

Zi–lu asked, "Have you seen my Master?"

The old man said, "You seem neither to have toiled with your limbs nor to be able to tell one kind of grain from another. Who may your Master be?" He planted his staff in the ground and started weeding.

Zi–lu stood, cupping one hand respectfully in the other.

The old man invited Zi–lu to stay for the night. He killed a chicken and prepared some millet for his guest to eat, and presented his two sons to him.

The next day, Zi–lu resumed his journey and reported this

挑着除草用的工具。

子路问道："您看见我的老师吗?"

老头道："你这人，四肢不劳动，五谷不认识，谁晓得你的老师是什么人?"说完，便扶着拐杖去锄草。

子路拱着手恭敬地站着。

他便留子路到他家住宿，杀鸡、做饭给子路吃，又叫他两个儿子出来相见。

第二天，子路赶上了孔子，报告了这件事。

孔子道："这是位隐士。"叫子路回去再看看他。子路到了那里，他却走开了。

子路便道："不做官是不对的。长幼间的关系，是不可能废弃的；君臣间的关系，怎么能不管呢?你原想不玷污自身，却不知道这样隐居便是忽视了君臣间的必要关系。君子出来做官，只是尽应尽之责。至于我们的政治主张行不通，早就知道了。"

8. **逸民：伯夷、叔齐、虞仲、夷逸、朱张、柳下惠、少连。子曰："不降其志，不辱其身，伯夷、叔齐与!"谓："柳下惠、少连，降志辱身矣，言中伦，行中虑，其斯而已矣。"谓："虞仲、夷逸，隐居放言，身中清，废中权。我则异于是，无可无不可。"**

conversation. The Master said, "He must be a recluse." He sent Zi-lu back to see him again. When he arrived, the old man had departed.

Zi-lu commented, "Not to enter public life is to ignore one's duty. Even the proper regulation of old and young cannot be set aside. How, then, can the duty between ruler and subject be set aside? This is to cause confusion in the most important of human relationships simply because one desired to keep unsullied one's character. The gentleman takes office in order to do his duty. As for putting the Way into practice, he knows all along that it is hopeless."[8]

8. Cf. XIV.38.

8. Men who withdrew from society: Bo Yi, Shu Qi, Yu Zhong, Yi Yi, Zhu Zhang, Liu Xia Hui, Shao Lian. The Master commented, "Not to lower their purpose or to allow themselves to be humiliated describes, perhaps, Bo Yi and Shu Qi." Of Liu Xia Hui and Shao Lian he said, "They, indeed, lowered their purpose and allowed themselves to be humiliated, but their

古今被遗落的人才有伯夷、叔齐、虞仲、夷逸、朱张、柳下惠、少连。孔子道："不动摇自己意志，不辱没自己身份，是伯夷、叔齐罢！"又说："柳下惠、少连降低自己意志，屈辱自己身份了，可是言语合乎法度，行为经过思虑，那也不过如此罢了。"又说："虞仲、夷逸逃世隐居，放肆直言。*行为廉洁，被废弃也是他的权术*。我就和他们这些人不同，没有什么可以，也没有什么不可以。"

9. 大师挚适齐，亚饭干适楚，三饭缭适蔡，四饭缺适秦，鼓方叔入于河，播鼗武入于汉，少师阳、击磬襄入于海。

太师挚逃到了齐国，二饭乐师干逃到了楚国，三饭乐师缭逃到了蔡国，四饭乐师缺逃到了秦国，打鼓的方叔入居黄河之滨，摇小鼓的武入居汉水之涯，少师阳和击磬的襄入居海边。

10. 周公谓鲁公曰："君子不施其亲，不使大臣怨乎不以。故旧无大故，则不弃也。无求备于一人！"

周公对鲁公说道："君子不怠慢他的亲族，不让大臣抱怨没被信用。老臣故人没有发生严重过失，就不要抛弃他。不

words were in accord with their station, and their deeds with circumspection. That was all." Of Yu Zhong and Yi Yi he said, "They lived as recluses and gave free rein to their words. *Thus they accorded, in their persons, with purity, and, in their words, with the right measure for the occasion.* I, however, am different. I have no preconceptions about the permissible and the impermissible."

9. Zhi, the Grand Musician, left for Qi; Gan, musician for the second course, left for Chu; Liao, musician for the third course, left for Cai; Que, musician for the fourth course, left for Qin; Fang Shu the drummer crossed the River; Wu, player of the handdrum, crossed the River Han; Yang, the Grand Musician's deputy, and Xiang who played the stone chimes crossed the sea.

10. The Duke of Zhou said to the Duke of Lu, [9] "The gentleman does not treat those closely related to him casually, nor does he give his high officials occasion for complaint because their advice was not heeded. Unless there are grave reasons, he does

要对某一人求全责备!”

11. 周有八士:伯达、伯适、仲突、仲忽、叔夜、叔夏、季随、季䯄。

周朝有八个有教养的人:伯达、伯适、仲突、仲忽、叔夜、叔夏、季随、季䯄。

not abandon officials of long standing. He does not look for all-round perfection in a single person.'[10]

9. his son.

10. Cf. XIII.25.

11. There were eight Gentlemen in Zhou: Bo Da, Bo Kuo, Zhong Tu, Zhong Hu, Shu Ye, Shu Xia, Ji Sui and Ji Gua.

子张篇第十九

1. 子张曰："士见危致命，见得思义，祭思敬，丧思哀，其可已矣。"

子张说："读书人看见危险便肯豁出生命，看见有所得便考虑是否该得，祭祀时候考虑严肃恭敬，居丧时候考虑悲痛哀伤，那也就可以了。"

2. 子张曰："执德不弘，信道不笃，焉能为有?焉能为亡?"

子张说："对于道德，行为不坚强，信仰不忠实，*[这种人，]有他不为多，没他不为少。*"

3. 子夏之门人问交于子张。

子张曰："子夏云何?"

对曰："子夏曰：'可者与之，其不可者拒之。'"

子张曰："异乎吾所闻:君子尊贤而容众，嘉善而矜不能。我之大贤与，于人何所不容?我之不贤与，人将拒我，如之何其拒人也?"

子夏的学生向子张问怎样去交朋友。子张道："子夏说了些什么?"

答道："子夏说，可以交的去交他，不可以交的拒绝他。"

子张道："我所听到的与此不同:君子尊敬贤人，也接纳普

BOOK 19

1. Zi-zhang said, "One can, perhaps, be satisfied with a Gentleman who is ready to lay down his life in the face of danger, who does not forget what is right at the sight of gain, [1] and who forgets neither reverence during a sacrifice nor sorrow while in mourning."

1. Cf. XIV、12.

2. Zi-zhang said, "*Wherein can a man be said either to have anything or not to have anything* who fails to hold on to virtue with all his might or to believe in the Way with all his heart."

3. Zi-xia's disciples asked Zi-zhang about friendship.

Zi-zhang said, "What does Zi-xia say?"

"Zi-xia says, 'You should make friends with those who are adequate and spurn those who are inadequate.'"

Zi-zhang said, "That is different from what I have heard. I have heard that the gentleman honours his betters and is tolerant towards the multitude and that he is full of praise for the good while taking pity on the backward. If I am greatly superior, which among men need I be intolerant of? If I am inferior, then others will spurn me, how can there be any question of my

通人；鼓励好人，可怜无能的人。我是非常好的人吗，对什么人不能容纳呢?我是坏人吗，别人会拒绝我，我怎能去拒绝别人呢?”

4. 子夏曰：“虽小道，必有可观者焉；致远恐泥，是以君子不为也。”

子夏说道：“就是小技艺，一定有可取的地方；恐怕它妨碍远大事业，所以君子不从事于它。”

5. 子夏曰：“日知其所亡，月无忘其所能，可谓好学也已矣。”

子夏说：“每天知道所未知的，每月复习所已能的，可以说是好学了。”

6. 子夏曰：“博学而笃志，切问而近思，仁在其中矣。”

子夏说：“广泛地学习，坚守自己志趣；恳切地发问，多考虑当前的问题，仁德就在这中间了。”

7. 子夏曰：“百工居肆以成其事，君子学以致其道。”

子夏说：“各种工人居住于其制造场所完成他们的工作，君子则用学习获得那个道。”

spurning them?"

4. Zi-xia said, "Even minor arts are sure to have their worthwhile aspects, but the gentleman does not take them up for fear of being bogged down when the way ahead is long."

5. Zi-xia said, "A man can, indeed, be said to be eager to learn who is conscious, in the course of a day, of what he lacks and who never forgets, in the course of a month, what he has mastered."

6. Zi-xia said, "Learn widely and be steadfast in your purpose, inquire earnestly and reflect on what is at hand, and there is no need for you to look for benevolence elsewhere."

7. Zi-xia said, "The artisan, in any of the hundred crafts, masters his trade by staying in his workshop; the gentleman perfects his way through learning."

8. 子夏曰："小人之过也必文。"

子夏说："小人对于错误一定加以掩饰。"

9. 子夏曰："君子有三变：望之俨然，即之也温，听其言也厉。"

子夏说："君子有三变：远远望着，庄严可畏；向他靠拢，温和可亲；听他的话，严厉不苟。"

10. 子夏曰："君子信而后劳其民；未信，则以为厉己也。信而后谏；未信，则以为谤己也。"

子夏说："君子必须得到信仰以后才去动员百姓；否则百姓会以为你在折磨他们。必须得到信任以后才去进谏，否则君上会以为你在毁谤他。"

11. 子夏曰："大德不逾闲，小德出入可也。"

子夏说："人的重大节操不能逾越界限，作风上的小节稍稍放松一点是可以的。"

12. 子游曰："子夏之门人小子，当洒扫应对进退，则可矣，抑末也。本之则无，如之何？"

8. Zi–xia said, "When the small man makes a mistake, he is sure to gloss over it."

9. Zi–xia said, "In the three following situations the gentleman gives a different impression. From a distance he appears formal; when approached, he appears cordial; in speech he appears stem."

10. Zi–xia said, "Only after he has gained the trust of the common people does the gentleman work them hard, for otherwise they would feel themselves ill–used. Only after he has gained the trust of the lord does the gentleman admonish him against wrong action, for otherwise the lord would feel himself slandered."

11. Zi–xia said, "If one does not overstep the bounds in major matters, it is of no consequence if one is not meticulous in minor matters."

12. Zi–you said, "The disciples and younger followers of Zi–xia can certainly cope with the task of sweeping and cleaning, of

子夏闻之，曰："噫！言游过矣！君子之道，孰先传焉？孰后倦焉？譬诸草木，区以别矣。君子之道，焉可诬也？有始有卒者，其惟圣人乎！"

子游道："子夏的学生，叫他们做做打扫、接待客人、应对进退的工作，那是可以的；不过这只是末节罢了。探讨他们的学术基础却没有，怎样可以呢？"

子夏听了这话，便道："咳！言游说错了！君子的学术，哪一项先传授呢？哪一项最后讲述呢？学术犹如草木，是要区别为各种各类的。君子的学术，如何可以歪曲？［依照一定的次序去传授而］有始有终的，大概只有圣人罢！"

13. 子夏曰："仕而优则学，学而优则仕。"

子夏说："做官了，有余力便去学习；学习了，有余力便去做官。"

responding to calls and replying to questions put to them, and of coming forward and withdrawing, but these are only trifling matters. On what is basic they are wanting. What can one do about this?"

When Zi-xia heard this, he said, "Oh! how mistaken Yan You is! In the way of the gentleman, what should be taught first and what should come afterwards are as clearly distinguished as grasses and trees. How can one give a false account of the way of the gentleman. It is, perhaps, the sage alone who, having started something, will always see it through to the end."[2]

2. Zi-xia's point seems to be this. If a student is taught, step by step, from the superficial to the basic, then he would have gained something even if he does not, in pursuing his studies, attain his final goal. At any rate, the final goal is something only the sage is supposed to be capable of attaining.

13. Zi-xia said, "When a man in office finds that he can more than cope with his duties, then he studies; when a student finds that he can more than cope with his studies, then he takes office."

子张篇第十九

14. 子游曰："丧致乎哀而止。"

子游说："居丧，充分表现了他的悲哀也就够了。"

15. 子游曰："吾友张也为难能也，然而未仁。"

子游说："我的朋友子张是难能可贵的了，然而还不能做到仁。"

16. 曾子曰："堂堂乎张也，难与并为仁矣。"

曾子说："子张的为人高得不可攀了，难以携带别人一同进入仁德。"

17. 曾子曰："吾闻诸夫子：人未有自致者也，必也亲丧乎！"

曾子说："我听老师说过，平常时候，人不可能来自动地充分发挥感情，[如果有，]一定在父母死亡的时候罢！"

18. 曾子曰："吾闻诸夫子：孟庄子之孝也，其他可能也；其不改父之臣与父之政，是难能也。"

曾子说："我听老师说过：孟庄子的孝，别的都容易做到；而留用他父亲的僚属，保持他父亲的政治设施，是难以做到的。"

BOOK 19

14. Zi-you said, "When mourning gives full expression to grief nothing more can be required."

15. Zi-you said, "My friend Zhang is difficult to emulate. All the same he has not, as yet, attained benevolence."

16. Zeng Zi said, "Grand, indeed, is Zhang, so much so that it is difficult to work side by side with him at the cultivation of benevolence."

17. Zeng Zi said, "I have heard the Master say that on no occasion does a man realize himself to the full, though, when pressed, he said that mourning for one's parents may be an exception."

18. Zeng Zi said, "I have heard the Master say that other men could emulate everything Meng Zhuang Zi did as a good son with the exception of one thing: he left unchanged both his father's officials and his father's policies, and this was what was difficult to emulate."[3]

3. Cf. Ⅰ.11.

19. 孟氏使阳肤为士师，问于曾子。曾子曰：“上失其道，民散久矣。如得其情，则哀矜而勿喜！”

孟氏任命阳肤做法官，阳肤向曾子求教。曾子道：“现今在上位的人不依规矩行事，百姓早就离心离德了。你假若能够审出罪犯的真情，便应该同情他，可怜他，切不要自鸣得意！”

20. 子贡曰：“纣之不善，不如是之甚也。是以君子恶居下流，天下之恶皆归焉。”

子贡说：“商纣的坏，不像现在传说的这么厉害。所以君子憎恨居于下流，一居下流，天下的什么坏名声都会集中在他身上了。”

21. 子贡曰：“君子之过也，如日月之食焉：过也，人皆见之；更也，人皆仰之。”

子贡说：“君子的过失好比日蚀月蚀：错误的时候，每个人都看得见；更改的时候，每个人都仰望着。”

22. 卫公孙朝问于子贡曰：“仲尼焉学？”

子贡曰：“文武之道，未坠于地，在人。贤者识其大者，不贤者识其小者。莫不有文武之道焉。夫子焉不学？而亦何常

BOOK 19

19. The Meng family appointed Yang Fu as judge and he sought the advice of Zeng Zi. Zeng Zi said, "Those in authority have lost the Way and the common people have, for long, been rootless. If you succeed in extracting the truth from them, you should have compassion on them instead of feeling pleased with yourself."

20. Zi-gong said, "Zhou was not as wicked as all that. That is why the gentleman hates to dwell downstream for it is there that all that is sordid in the Empire finds its way."

21. Zi-gong said, "The gentleman's errors are like an eclipse of the sun and the moon in that when he errs the whole world sees it and when he reforms the whole world looks up to it."

22. Gong-sun Chao of Wei asked Zi-gong, "From whom did Zhong-ni[4] learn?"

Zi-gong said, "The way of King Wen and King Wu has not

师之有？”

卫国的公孙朝向子贡问道：“孔仲尼的学问是从哪里学来的？”子贡道：“周文王、武王之道，并没有失传，散在人间。贤能的人便抓住大处，不贤能的人只抓些末节。没有地方没有文王、武王之道。我的老师何处不学，又为什么要有一定的老师，专门的传授呢？”

23. 叔孙武叔语大夫于朝曰：“子贡贤于仲尼。”

子服景伯以告子贡。

子贡曰：“譬之宫墙，赐之墙也及肩，窥见室家之好。夫子之墙数仞，不得其门而入，不见宗庙之美，百官之富。得其门者或寡矣。夫子之云，不亦宜乎！”

叔孙武叔在朝廷中对官员们说：“子贡比他老师仲尼要强些。”

子服景伯便把这话告诉子贡。

子贡道：“拿房屋的围墙作比喻罢：我家的围墙只有肩膀那么高，谁都可以探望到房屋的美好。我老师的围墙却有几丈高，找不到大门走进去，就看不到他那宗庙的雄伟，房舍的多种多样。能够找着大门的人或许不多罢，那么，武叔他老

yet fallen to the ground but is still to be found in men. There is no man who does not have something of the way of Wen and Wu in him. Superior men have got hold of what is of greater significance while inferior men have got hold of what is of lesser significance. From whom, then, does the Master not learn? Equally, how could there be such a thing as a constant teacher for him?"

4. i.e., Confucius.

23. Shu-sun Wu-shu said to the Counsellors at court, "Zi-gong is superior to Zhong-ni."

This was reported to Zi-gong by Zi-fu Jing-bo.

Zi-gong said, "Let us take outer walls as an analogy. My walls are shoulder high so that it is possible to peer over them and see the beauty of the house. But the Master's walls are twenty or thirty feet high so that, unless one gains admittance through the gate, one cannot see the magnificence of the ancestral temples or the sumptuousness of the official buildings. Since those who gain admittance through the gate are, shall we say, few, is it any wonder that the gentleman should have spoken as he did?"

人家的这话，不也是自然的吗?”

24. 叔孙武叔毁仲尼。子贡曰：“无以为也!仲尼不可毁也。他人之贤者，丘陵也，犹可逾也；仲尼，日月也，无得而逾焉。人虽欲自绝，其何伤于日月乎?多见其不知量也。”

叔孙武叔毁谤仲尼。子贡道：“不要这样做！仲尼是毁谤不了的。别人的贤能，好比山丘，还可以超越过去；仲尼，简直是太阳和月亮，不可能超越他。人家纵是要自绝于太阳月亮，那对太阳月亮有什么损害呢?只是表示他不自量罢了。”

25. 陈子禽谓子贡曰：“子为恭也，仲尼岂贤于子乎?”

子贡曰：“君子一言以为知，一言以为不知，言不可不慎也。夫子之不可及也，犹天之不可阶而升也。夫子之得邦家者，所谓立之斯立，道之斯行，绥之斯来，动之斯和。其生也荣，其死也哀，如之何其可及也?”

陈子禽对子贡道：“您对仲尼是客气罢，是谦让罢，难道他真比您还强吗?”

子贡道：“高贵人物由一句话表现他的有知，也由一句话表现他的无知，所以说话不可不谨慎。他老人家的不可以赶得上，犹如青天的不可以用阶梯爬上去。他老人家如果得国

BOOK 19

24. Shu–sun Wu–shu made defamatory remarks about Zhong–ni. Zi–gong said, "He is simply wasting his time. Zhong–ni cannot be defamed. In other cases, men of excellence are like hills which one can climb over. Zhong–ni is like the sun and the moon which one has no way of climbing over. Even if someone wanted to cut himself off from them, how could this detract from the sun and the moon.? It would merely serve to show that he did not know his own measure."

25. Chen Zi–qin said to Zi–gong, "You are just being respectful, aren't you? Surely Zhong–ni is not superior to you."

Zi–gong said, "The gentleman is judged wise by a single word he utters; equally, he is judged foolish by a single word he utters. That is why one really must be careful of what one says. The Master cannot be equalled just as the sky cannot be scaled. Were the Master to become the head of a state or a noble family, he would be like the man described in the saying: he only has to help them stand and they will stand, to guide them and they will walk, to bring peace to them and they will

而为诸侯，或者得到采邑而为卿大夫，那正如我们所说的一叫百姓人人能立足于社会，百姓自会人人能立足于社会；一引导百姓，百姓自会前进；一安抚百姓，百姓自会从远方来投靠；一动员百姓，百姓自会同心协力。他老人家，生得光荣，死得可惜，怎么样能够赶得上呢？”

turn to him, to set them tasks and they will work in harmony. In life he is honoured and in death he will be mourned. How can he be equalled?"

尧曰篇第二十

1. 尧曰："咨！尔舜！天之历数在尔躬，允执其中。四海困穷，天禄永终。"

舜亦以命禹。

曰："予小子履敢用玄牡，敢昭告于皇皇后帝：有罪不敢赦。帝臣不蔽，简在帝心。朕躬有罪，无以万方；万方有罪，罪在朕躬。"

周有大赉，善人是富。"虽有周亲，不如仁人。百姓有过，在予一人。"

谨权量，审法度，修废官，四方之政行焉。兴灭国，继绝世，举逸民，天下之民归心焉。

所重：民、食、丧、祭。

宽则得众，信则民任焉，敏则有功，公则说。

尧［让位给舜的时候，］说道："啧啧！你这位舜！上天的大命已经落到你的身上了，诚实地保持着那正确罢！假若天下的百姓都陷于困苦贫穷，上天给你的禄位也会永远地终止了。"

舜［让位给禹的时候，］也说了这一番话。

［汤］说："我履谨用黑色牡牛作牺牲，明明白白地告于光明而伟大的天帝：有罪的人［我］不敢擅自去赦免他。您的臣仆［的善恶］我也不隐瞒掩盖，您心里也是早就晓得的。我本人若有罪，就不要牵连天下万方；天下万方若有罪，都归

BOOK 20

1. Yao said,

Oh, Shun,

The succession, ordained by Heaven, has fallen on thy person.

Holdst thou truly to the middle way.

If the Empire should be reduced to dire straits

The honours bestowed on thee by Heaven will be terminated for ever.

Shun commanded Yu in like manner.

[Tang] said, "I, Lü, the little one, dare to offer a black bull and to make this declaration before the great Lord. I dare not pardon those who have transgressed. I shall present thy servants as they are so that the choice rests with Thee alone. If I transgress, let not the ten thousand states suffer because of me; but if the ten thousand states transgress, the guilt is mine alone."

The Chou handed out great gifts and good men alone were enriched.

I may have close relatives,

But better for me to have benevolent men.

我一个人来承担。”

周朝大封诸侯，使善人都富贵起来。“我虽然有至亲，却不如有仁德之人。百姓如果有罪过，应该由我来担承。”

检验并审定度量衡，修复已废弃的机关工作，全国的政令就都会通行了。恢复被灭亡的国家，承续已断绝的后代，提拔被遗落的人才，天下的百姓就都会心悦诚服了。

所重视的:人民、粮食、丧礼、祭祀。

宽厚就会得到群众的拥护，勤敏就会有功绩，公平就会使百姓高兴。

BOOK 20

If the people transgress

Let my person be punished.[1]

Decide on standard weights and measures after careful consideration, and re-establish official posts fallen into disuse, and government measures will be enforced everywhere. Restore states that have been annexed, revive lines that have become extinct, raise men who have withdrawn from society and the hearts of all the common people in the Empire will turn to you.

What was considered of importance: the common people, food, mourning and sacrifice.

If a man is tolerant, he will win the multitude. If he is trustworthy in word, the common people will entrust him with responsibility. If he is quick he will achieve results.[2] If he is impartial the common people will be pleased.[3]

1. It has been suggested that these are the words used by King Wu in enfeoffing feudal lords, and may have been used, in particular, in the enfeoffment of Tai Gong of Qi.

 This whole passage consists of advice to kings or declarations by them. These kings all founded new dynasties. Shun founded the Yu 虞, Yu禹 founded the Xia 夏, Tang 汤 founded the Yin 殷, and King Wu founded the Zhou. It must have been taken from the *Book of His–*

尧曰篇第二十

2. 子张问于孔子曰："何如斯可以从政矣？"

子曰："尊五美，屏四恶，斯可以从政矣。"

子张曰："何谓五美？"

子曰："君子惠而不费，劳而不怨，欲而不贪，泰而不骄，威而不猛。"

子张曰："何谓惠而不费？"

子曰："因民之所利而利之，斯不亦惠而不费乎？择可劳而劳之，又谁怨？欲仁而得仁，又焉贪？君子无众寡，无小大，无敢慢，斯不亦泰而不骄乎？君子正其衣冠，尊其瞻视，俨然人望而畏之，斯不亦威而不猛乎？"

子张曰："何谓四恶？"

tory, although only the saying of Tang is found quoted in ancient works. This kind of material was probably used for teaching purposes in the Confucian school.

2. The paragraph up to this point is also found in XVII.6 where instead of *min* (common people) the text reads *ren* (fellow men).
3. This passage is not attributed to any speaker. It seems to consist of a number of unconnected parts on various aspects of government. Although one of these parts, as we have just pointed out, is, indeed, attributed to Confucius in XVII.6, it would be rash to infer from this that Confucius must have been responsible for everything else as well.

2. Zi-zhang asked Confucius, "What must a man be like before he can take part in government?"

The Master said, "If he exalts the five excellent practices and eschews the four wicked practices he can take part in government."

Zi-zhang said, "What is meant by the five excellent practices?"

The Master said, "The gentleman is generous without its costing him anything, works others hard without their complaining, has desires without being greedy, is at ease without being arrogant, and is awe-inspiring without looking fierce."

尧曰篇第二十

子曰："不教而杀谓之虐；不戒视成谓之暴；慢令致期谓之贼；犹之与人也，出纳之吝谓之有司。"

子张向孔子问道："怎样就可以治理政事呢？"

孔子道："尊贵五种美德，排除四种恶政，这就可以治理政事了。"

子张道："五种美德是些什么？"

孔子道："君子给人民以好处，而自己却无所耗费；劳动百姓，百姓却不怨恨；自己欲仁欲义，却不能叫做贪；安泰矜持却不骄傲；威严却不凶猛。"

子张道："给人民以好处，自己却无所耗费，这应该怎么办呢？"

孔子道："就着人民能得利益之处因而使他们有利，这也不是给人民以好处而自己却无所耗费吗？选择可以劳动的［时间、情况和人民］再去劳动他们，又有谁来怨恨呢？自己需要仁德便得到了仁德，又贪求什么呢？无论人多人少，无论势力大小，君子都不敢怠慢他们，这不也是安泰矜持却不骄傲吗？君子衣冠整齐，目不邪视，庄严地使人望而有所畏惧，这不也是威严却不凶猛吗？"

子张道："四种恶政又是些什么呢？"

孔子道："不加教育便加杀戮叫做虐；不加申诫便要成绩叫做暴；起先懈怠，突然限期叫做贼；同是给人以财物，出

BOOK 20

Zi-zhang said, "What is meant by 'being generous without its costing him anything'?"[4]

The Master said, "If a man benefits the common people by taking advantage of the things around them that they find beneficial, is this not being generous without its costing him anything? If a man, in working others hard, chooses burdens they can support, who will complain.? If, desiring benevolence, a man obtains it, where is the greed? The gentleman never dare neglect his manners whether he be dealing with the many or the few, the young or the old. Is this not being at ease without being arrogant?[5] The gentleman, with his robe and cap adjusted properly and dignified in his gaze, has a presence which inspires people who see him with awe. Is this not being awe-inspiring without looking fierce?"

Zi-zhang said, "What is meant by the four wicked practices?"

The Master said, "To impose the death penalty without first reforming the people is to be cruel; to expect results without first giving warning is to be tyrannical; to insist on a time limit when tardy in issuing orders is to cause injury. When something has to be given to others anyway, to be miserly in the ac-

手悭吝，叫做小家子气。”

3. 孔子曰：“不知命，无以为君子也；不知礼，无以立也；不知言，无以知人也。”

孔子说：“不懂得命运，没有可能作为君子；不懂得礼，没有可能立足于社会；不懂得分辨人家的言语，没有可能认识人。”

tual giving is to be officious."

4. In the light of the answer, the question should cover all five excellent practices instead of only the first.

5. Cf. XIII.26.

3. Confucius said, "A man has no way of becoming a gentleman unless he understands Destiny; he has no way of taking his stand unless he understands the rites;[6] he has no way of judging men unless he understands words."

6. Cf. VIII.8, XVI.13.